Thames Ring
and London Ring Atlas

RIVER THAMES

Contents

Designed, written and produced by GEOprojects (UK) Limited.

Maps based upon Ordnance Survey mapping with the permission of the Controller of Her Majesty's Stationery Office. © Crown copyright (43372U).

All possible care was taken in the preparation of this atlas, and whilst the publishers would be grateful to learn of any errors, they regret they can accept no responsibility for any inaccuracies and for any expense or loss thereby caused.

The representation on these maps of any road, path or open space is no evidence of the existence of a right of way.

Cover photograph: River Thames, Cookham, Berks. Supplied and reproduced by kind permission of Ian Meredith.

Other photographs reproduced by kind permission of British Waterways Photographic Library, Derek Pratt (Waterways Photo Library) and Harry Arnold (Waterway Images Limited).

GEOprojects (UK) Limited would like to acknowledge the help and co-operation given by British Waterways, the Countryside Commission and the Environment Agency in the preparation of the maps.

Printed by Bookbuilders Ltd, Hong Kong.
727

GEOprojects (UK) Ltd,
9-10, Southern Court,
South Street,
Reading,
Berkshire,
RG1 4QS
Tel: 0118 939 3567
Fax: 0118 959 8283

GEO projects

An Introduction to the Thames Ring

The Thames Ring includes parts of the Oxford Canal, River Thames and Grand Union Canal. A total of 256 miles of navigable waterway passing through diverse scenery, from the remote Oxfordshire countryside to the bustle of London. At a relaxed cruising pace the ring should be completed in about 3 weeks but it can also be enjoyed by walking the towpath, taking a cruise or sampling one of the many waterside pubs.

The Thames Ring Atlas features fully revised and updated GEOprojects mapping in a convenient format. Each section includes information on boatyards and useful addresses and telephone numbers. The popular, award winning maps show the waterway corridor in detail with facilities available to the boat-user, footpaths, pubs and other features of interest.

Boating Information

Three important facts should be known before attempting to cruise the whole of the Thames and London Rings.
1) Beam: a complete circumnavigation is only possible in craft of no wider than 6'10" (2.08m), the maximum recommended beam for boats using the Oxford Canal between Napton and Oxford where the locks are all narrow gauge, i.e. no more than 7' wide.
2) Licensing: for craft normally registered with British Waterways an extra license fee is charged when passing onto the River Thames which is administered by the Environment Agency and vice versa. Information on registration and licensing can be obtained at the addresses shown below.
3) Tideway experience: as the River Thames is tidal down river of Teddington, boaters are advised not to attempt the journey between Teddington and Brentford, or to Limehouse, without previous tideway navigation experience and without contacting the authorities listed below.

Some of the marina facilities listed in the tables on pages 6, 16, 17 and 31, may be for private use by the marina's long term moorers. Please check with each marina on the availability of facilities to non-moorers.

Navigation Authorities, Registration and Licensing

Grand Union and Oxford Canals
These canals are owned and managed by British Waterways. As far as the Thames and London Rings are concerned navigation is the responsibility of the waterway managers based at the following British Waterways offices: Braunston (Oxford Canal and Grand Union Canal between Napton Junction and Stowe Hill), Marsworth (Grand Union Canal between Stowe Hill and Uxbridge) and Little Venice (Grand Union Canal between Uxbridge and Limehouse).

British Waterways
The Stop House
Braunston
Northamptonshire
NN11 7JQ
Tel: 01788 890666

British Waterways
Marsworth Junction
Watery Lane
Marsworth
Tring
Hertfordshire
HP23 4LZ
Tel: 01442 825938

British Waterways
The Toll Office
Delamere Terrace
London
W2 6ND
Tel: 0171 286 6101

All craft using the Grand Union and Oxford Canals must display a British Waterways license and visitor licenses are available for craft not normally resident on BW waterways, obtainable from the waterway offices listed above and from the lock-keeper at Thames Lock, Brentford, Tel: 0181 560 1120 and the British Waterways Harbour Master's Office at
Limehouse Ship Lock:
Limehouse Basin
Narrow Street
London
E14 8DN
Tel: 0171 895 9930

For full details of transitting Thames or Limehouse Ship Locks for passage between the Grand Union Canal and the Thames tideway contact British Waterways staff at Brentford or Limehouse.

River Thames
The navigation authority for the freshwater Thames, above Teddington, is the Environment Agency Thames Region based in Reading with local navigation inspectors based at Oxford, Reading, Maidenhead and Sunbury.

All vessels on the River Thames must be registered and licensed with the Environment Agency and visiting craft may obtain short period certificates. Details of craft registration, licensing and navigational information can be obtained from:
Environment Agency
Kings Meadow House
Kings Meadow Road
Reading
Berkshire
RG1 8DQ
Tel: 0118 953 5000

The Environment Agency publish *A User's Guide to the River Thames* giving general information, regulations and information about facilities on the river, available from the address above.

Teddington Locks are manned 24 hours each day of the year and the lock-keeper can be contacted on tel: 0181 940 8723.

Navigation on the Thames below Teddington is the responsibility of the Port of London Authority (PLA). Private pleasure craft using the upper tideway do not require a license but all vessels must be navigated in accordance with the Port of London Authority Byelaws. *The Tidal Thames a pleasure users guide*, published by the PLA should be read in advance of a tidal passage and is obtainable, together with other information, from:
Port of London Authority
Devon House
58-60 St Katharine's Way
London
E1 9LB
Tel: 0171 265 2656

Navigational Notes and Warnings

The speed limit for craft on the Grand Union and Oxford Canals is 4 mph (6.4 km/hr).

The speed limit for powered craft on the River Thames upstream of Teddington is 5 mph (8km/hr).

Keep all wash to a minimum by maintaining a steady speed below the allowed limit.

A breaking wash created by powered boats will erode bank sides. All powered craft should keep to the centre of the canal.

Pass moored craft and fishermen at a steady slow speed.

All powered craft using the Grand Union and Oxford Canals will require a British Waterways windlass to operate the locks, obtainable from British Waterways.

Upstream traffic should give way to downstream traffic on fast flowing sections of river.

Approach sharp turns, junctions and bridge-holes with caution.

Pass oncoming vessels port side to port side, ie left-hand side to left-hand side.

Journey Planner

Broad canal (over 7ft wide)

Broad canal - no longer navigable

Narrow canal (max 7ft wide)

Narrow canal - no longer navigable

River Navigation

Tidal river navigation

4〈 Lock flight with number of locks

Tunnel

◇ Feature of interest

12M / 8L Distance in miles / number of locks between markers

▲80 Height of waterway in feet above sea-level

Coventry Canal

Ashby de la Zouch Canal

COVENTRY

Oxford Canal

RUGBY

Grand Union Canal

Braunston Turn to Coventry 28 miles

Norton Junction to Leicester 41 miles

Gayton Junction to Peterborough 66 miles

Market Harborough Arm

MARKET HARBOROUGH

WATFORD

Braunston Turn
5M / 0L
320

BRAUNSTON
6
320

Braunston Marina
4½M / 6L
360

Norton Junction
7

12¼M / 7L

NORTHAMPTON

River Nene

Napton Junction

← Napton Junction to Birmingham 36 miles

9 NAPTON ON THE HILL

DAVENTRY

WEEDON BEC

STOWE HILL

Northampton Arm

Gayton Junction
290▲

BLISWORTH

Meandering Canal

Summit Level 384 ▲

11½M / 9L

◇ Fenny Compton Tunnel

FENNY COMPTON

6¾M / 9L ↗5

CROPREDY

◇ Blisworth Tunnel

STOKE BRUERNE

◇ The Canal Museum
7

10½M / 7L

Grand Union Canal

4½M / 4L

Tooley's Boatyard ◇

BANBURY

6¾M / 4L

AYNHO

6M / 3L

UPPER HEYFORD

LOWER HEYFORD

Cosgrove Junction
▲230

COSGROVE

OLD STRATFORD

Old Stratford Arm

NEWPORT PAGNELL

Newport Pagnell Canal

Buckingham Arm

250▲

BUCKINGHAM

MILTON KEYNES

11¼M / 1L

Thames Ring

Oxford Canal

7¾M / 5L

Fenny Stratford

3

8M / 6L

LINSLADE

LEIGHTON BUZZARD

◇ Thrupp

3½M / 3L KIDLINGTON

Duke's Cut

3M / 2L

200▲

Sheepwash Channel

OXFORD

8M / 11L

Aylesbury Arm

Marsworth Junction

AYLESBURY
250▲

Tring Reservoirs

◇

Wendover Arm
390▲
WENDOVER

Bulbourne Junction

MARSWORTH

395▲ Tring Summit Level

TRING

6½M / 14L

BERKHAMSTED

HEMEL HEMPSTEAD

7M / 17L

KINGS LANGLEY

7M / 13L WATFORD

BISHOP'S STORTFORD

Stort Navigation

HERTFORD

HARLOW

Lee Navigation

Sandford Lock ◇

ABINGDON
160▲

River Thames

← Duke's Cut to Lechlade 27½ miles

Wilts & Berks Canal

DORCHESTER

15M / 4L

WALLINGFORD

7¾M / 4L

CHILTERN HILLS

6M / 2L

Goring Gap ◇
GORING

10M / 2L

PANGBOURNE

◇ Mapledurham Mill

9¾M / 4L

CAVERSHAM
130▲

SONNING

Kennet Mouth

READING

8M / 3L MARLOW

◇ Henley Reach

HENLEY-ON-THAMES

13¾M / 5L

MAIDENHEAD

◇ Maidenhead Railway Bridge

SLOUGH

WINDSOR

Kennet and Avon Canal

NEWBURY

← Kennet Mouth to Bath 77 miles

DENHAM

Cowley Peachey Junction
110▲

UXBRIDGE
110▲

Slough Arm
110▲

9¾M / 8L

WEMBLEY

London Ring

◇ Little Venice
Regent's Canal

Paddington Arm

5¾M / 6L

11L

3¾M / 0L Bull's Bridge Junction

BRENTFORD

London Canal Museum

3

LIMEHOUSE

LONDON

3M / 0L

13¾M / 2L

WANDSWORTH

◇ Teddington Locks

Teddington Locks

11¼M / 5L

◇ London Stone

TEDDINGTON

13¾M / 2L

KINGSTON UPON THAMES

EGHAM

STAINES

SUNBURY

CHERTSEY
50▲

WEYBRIDGE

13M / 4L

River Thames

Basingstoke Canal

BASINGSTOKE

GUILDFORD

Wey Navigation

Scale 1:625 000

0   10 miles

0   10   20 kilometres

© GEOprojects 1997

Holiday Hiring

It is possible to cruise the Oxford and Grand Union Canals and the River Thames by hiring a boat from one of 35 hire bases on or adjacent to the Thames Ring with a wide range of craft and holiday options available. The hire bases below all feature on the maps in the atlas and are listed from north to south or upstream to downstream. Permission from the hire operator must be gained before entering the tidal Thames.

Grand Union Canal

Warwickshire Fly Boat Company, tel: 01926 812093......Stockton
Calcutt Boats, tel: 01926 813757 ....Calcutt Locks
Braunston Boats, tel: 01788 891079................................Braunston
Adventure Fleet / Union Canal Carriers,
        tel: 01788 890784..Braunston
Weltonfield Narrowboats, tel: 01327 842282 ....Welton Hythe
Canalboat Holidays (at Concoform Marine),
        tel: 01327 340739...Weedon
Alvechurch Boat Centres, tel: 01604 858685 ....Gayton Marina
Blisworth Tunnel Boats, tel: 01604 858868....................Blisworth
Wyvern Shipping Company, tel: 01525 372355...............Linslade
Bridgewater Boats, tel: 01442 863615.............................Berkhamsted
Adelaide Marine, tel: 0181 571 5678 ....Southall
Capital Canal Cruising, tel: 0181 842 0383....................Yeading

Oxford Canal

Napton Narrowboats, tel: 01926 813644 ....Napton Marina
Black Prince Holidays, tel: 01527 575115 ....Napton Marina

Sovereign Narrowboats, tel: 01295 275657 ....Banbury
Anglo Welsh Waterway Holidays, tel: 0117 924 1200.....Aynho Wharf
Oxfordshire Narrowboats, tel: 01869 340348..................Lower Heyford
College Cruisers, tel: 01865 54343 ....Oxford

River Thames

Oxford Cruisers, tel: 01865 881698 ....Eynsham
Kingcraft (at Abingdon Boat Centre),
        tel: 01235 521125...Abingdon
Red Line Cruisers, tel: 01235 535878 ....Abingdon
Benson Pleasure Craft, tel: 01491 838304......................Benson
Maidline Cruisers, tel: 01491 836088 ....Wallingford
Bridge Boats, tel: 0118 959 0346 ....Reading
Caversham Boat Services, tel: 0118 957 4323................Reading
Berry Brook Boats, tel: 0118 947 3184 ....Reading
Swancraft, tel: 0118 940 2577...Wargrave
Bourne End Marina, tel: 01628 522813..........................Bourne End
Kris Cruisers, tel: 01753 543930....................................Datchet
Chambers Boatyard, tel: 01784 482051...........................Hythe End
Aquamarine Boats, tel: 01784 456310............................Egham
Harris Boatbuilders, tel: 01932 563111.........................Laleham
Vjera Line Cruises, tel: 01392 252520 ....Walton-on-Thames
T W Allen & Son, tel: 0181 979 1997.............................East Molesey
Ferryline Cruisers, tel: 0181 398 0271 ....Thames Ditton

Walking

Using the appropriate sections of the Oxford Canal Walk and the Grand Union Canal Walk, following the canals' towpaths, and the Thames Path (the country's only long distance footpath to follow a river throughout its length) it is possible to walk the Thames Ring, although not always following the water's edge.

These paths are a legacy of Britain's industrial past. Two hundred years ago waterways transport was horse powered and horses required a towpath next to the canals and rivers along which they could haul boats.

Walking north from Oxford towards Braunston and following the Thames Ring to Brentford, the towpaths are continuous, leaving the canalside only at Braunston and Blisworth Tunnels where the recommended routes follow the former horse-paths over the tops of the tunnels. The route of the Thames Path shown on the maps follows the official route of the Countryside Commission's National Trail opened in July 1996. Temporary alternative routes with detours away from the river are shown at Cholsey, Purley-on-Thames, Shiplake and Datchet and it is not certain when these sections of path will be granted.

At Braunston Turn, the Oxford and Grand Union Canals and their towpaths meet. Walkers will need to cross the footbridge here.

Downstream of Teddington Lock Cut Footbridge the Thames Path has two official routes on the north and south banks with regular opportunities to cross over. The Thames Path meets the Grand Union Canal Walk at Bridge 209 on the canal at Brentford. The waymarked Thames Path briefly follows the A315 before turning towards Syon House, continuing through Syon Park to join the north bank of the river at Isleworth. The first crossings can be made at Richmond.

In Oxford the link between the Thames Path and the Oxford Canal Walk, keeping to the waters' edge, follows Sheepwash Channel (see the Oxford street plan on page 14). An alternative is to leave the Thames Path at Osney Bridge and pass the railway station towards the city centre to the start of the

Oxford Canal Walk on Hythe Bridge Street.

In the towns and urban areas the towpaths are generally in very good condition, often paved or with an improved surface, while in between they resemble country paths which can be muddy in the winter or after heavy rain, so appropriate footwear should be worn.

The Thames Path is well served by railway stations and the close proximity of the railway from Banbury southwards on the Oxford Canal and from Wolverton (near Milton Keynes) southwards on the Grand Union Canal facilitates walkers' access to parts of the Thames Ring.

Canal and riverside pubs regularly punctuate the route giving ample refreshment opportunity. Accommodation details and lists of local events and things to see and do can be obtained from the Tourist Information Centres listed below.

Tourist Information Centres

Grand Union Canal

Daventry, tel: 01327 300277
Milton Keynes, tel: 01908 232525
Hemel Hempstead, tel: 01442 234222
Hillingdon, tel: 01895 250706
Islington, tel: 0171 278 8787

Oxford Canal

Banbury, tel: 01295 259855
Woodstock, tel: 01993 811038
Oxford, tel: 01865 726871

River Thames

Abingdon, tel: 01235 522711
Wallingford, tel: 01491 826972
Reading, tel: 0118 956 6226
Henley-on-Thames,
    tel: 01491 578034
Marlow, tel: 01628 483597
Maidenhead, tel: 01628 781110
Windsor, tel: 01753 852010
Twickenham, tel: 0181 891 1411
Richmond, tel: 0181 940 9125

Blue Anchor, Hammersmith, on the route of the Thames Path   *Derek Pratt*

Map Reference

Waterway information

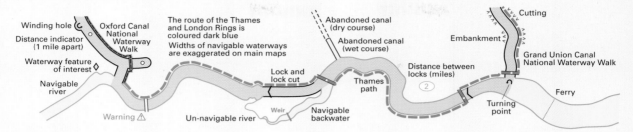

Boat user information

⊤	Long term mooring (Environment Agency and local authority mooring on Thames)	■	Boatyard	🛢	Refuse disposal
⊤	Temporary/overnight mooring	⤙	Slipway or public launch site	⊖	Elsan/sewage disposal
		🚰	Water point	P	Pump out

Tourist information

🛈	Tourist information centre	☺	Sports/leisure centre	⌐	Golf course
✝	Church of interest	⋰	Site of historic interest	▲	Youth hostel
🏰	Castle	•	Other feature of interest	✳	Boat trip
🏛	Historic house/building	ⵊ	Country park	⚓	Day boat hire
✻	Garden	🐦	Nature reserve	⚓	Holiday boat hire
◉	Museum	🎋	Picnic site	⚐	Water sports
▥	Theatre	🚌	Caravan site		
◉◉	Cinema	Ⱥ	Camping site		

General map information

M25	Motorway and junction number	▬▬▬	Railway and station	🚌	Bus station
A34	'A' road/dual carriageway	▬▬▬	County boundary	P	Car park
	Other road/dual carriageway	▤ Built-up area		T	Toilets
	Restricted access road	▤ Park/woodland		PO	Post office
- - - -	Path	▬▬▬ Main shopping area		☏	Telephone
				•	Public house
				▲	Hill

About the atlas

• The routes of the Thames Ring and the London Ring are coloured dark blue.

• On the main maps the width of the navigable waterways have been exaggerated so that on some sections of river, islands which are geographically mid-stream may appear displaced on the map. On the accompanying street plans the canal and river widths are to scale.

• The Oxford Canal maps are at a scale of 1:56,500 and the Thames and Grand Union Canal maps are at 1:60,000 with scale bars conveniently shown on each double page spread.

• On the Oxford and Grand Union Canal maps distance indicators are shown, one mile apart, while on the Thames maps distances in miles between locks are shown.

• North is indicated on each map.

• For the routes connecting the Thames and London Rings to the neighbouring waterways, please see the journey planner map on page 3.

Other waterway maps available:-

■ Basingstoke Canal
■ Birmingham Canal Navigations
■ The Broads
■ Caledonian Canal & the Great Glen
■ Grand Union Canal
   Map 1   Birmingham to Fenny Stratford
   Map 2   Braunston to Kings Langley
   Map 3   Fenny Stratford to the Thames
   Map 4   Leicester Line, Soar Navigation
           and Erewash Canal
■ Kennet & Avon Canal
■ Llangollen & Montgomery Canals
■ Oxford Canal
■ Shropshire Union Canal
■ Thames, *the river and the path*

and our national route planner:-

■ Inland Waterways of Britain

Oxford Canal

OXFORD CANAL | GRAND UNION CANAL

RIVER THAMES

The Oxford Canal section of the Thames Ring from Braunston to Oxford is just over 54 miles (87 km) long and has 39 narrow locks. Heading west from Braunston, the canal passes from Northamptonshire to Warwickshire before turning south at Napton on the Hill. Here the Napton Flight of 9 locks lifts the Oxford to its summit level between Marston Doles and Claydon, from where the canal descends into Oxfordshire via the Claydon Flight to follow the Cherwell Valley all the way to the River Thames and its terminus in the historic, university city of Oxford.

History

Proposers of the Oxford Canal envisaged a continuation of a line southwards from the Coventry Canal, authorised in 1768, to carry Warwickshire coal to London, via the Thames. In 1769 the Oxford Canal's Act of authorisation passed through Parliament and received its Royal Assent from George III. James Brindley (1716-1772), one of the most prolific canal builders, was appointed chief engineer and although he died before it was completed, his indelible stamp was left on the Oxford Canal. The canal's meandering course is entirely typical of his famous 'contour canals', designed to minimize the use of locks and avoid the need for expensive embankments, cuttings and tunnels. (Sections of the North Oxford Canal between Hawkesbury and Braunston were straightened in the period 1828-1834 to reduce journey times to improve the canal's commercial competitiveness.)

The canal was completed to Oxford on 1st January 1790 under the supervision of Brindley's brother-in-law, Samuel Simcock. Its first link with the River Thames was Duke's Cut, built by the Duke of Marlborough, a large share holder in the Oxford Canal, and opened in 1789; this was leased to the canal company from 1798. It was not until 1796 that the Oxford Canal Company had its own junction with the Thames through Isis Lock and Sheepwash Channel.

The opening of the Grand Junction Canal (now Grand Union) from Braunston to London in 1800 began a commercial rivalry between the two navigations which put the Oxford under considerable pressure but, with aggressive management, it remained profitable for many years despite this and, increasingly in the 19th century, competition with the railways. Commercial carrying ceased during the 1950s. Following this the section of canal between Napton and Oxford was threatened with closure and a rigorous campaign was successfully mounted to save the canal. The scenic and historic setting of the Oxford Canal soon attracted a new generation of pleasure boats and since 1962 British Waterways, the navigation authority, has encouraged a wide range of leisure activities on the canal.

Look out for

◊ **Meandering course** The Oxford Canal's most pronounced meander occurs on its summit level around Wormleighton Hill where a 3 mile (4.5 km) stretch loops back to 950 yards (868 metres) from its starting point.

◊ **Fenny Compton Tunnel** At Fenny Compton there is a long, steep-sided cutting, still anomalously known as Fenny Compton Tunnel, the roof of the tunnel having been removed in 1866.

◊ **Tooley's Boatyard** This historic boatyard was established in Banbury in 1790 to build narrowboats, 72' by 7', on what was one of the first standard gauge narrow canals.

◊ **Thrupp** A purpose built village which grew up with the canal, the cottages which look out onto the water-front are evidence of the prosperity brought by the Oxford Canal. Just to the north the canal is enlivened by the picturesque River Cherwell which forms the course of the canal.

Marina and Boatyard Facilities
Napton to Oxford

	Long term mooring	Temporary/over-night mooring	Slipway	Water	Refuse disposal	Elsan disposal	Pump out	Electricity points	Bottled gas	Diesel	Boat/engine repairs	Cranage	Hardstanding	Parts and equipment	Boat sales	Chandlery/shop
Napton Narrowboats Tel: 01926 813644	■	■		■	■	■	■	■	■	■				■	■	■
Cowroast Tel: 01295 770461	■	■		■	■	■	■	■	■	■				■	■	■
Sovereign Narrowboats Tel: 01295 275657	■	■		■				■	■							
Morse Marine Tel: 01295 261221	■	■					■		■	■	■	■		■	■	■
Aynho Wharf Boatbuilders Tel: 01869 338483	■	■		■	■	■	■	■	■	■				■		■
Oxfordshire Narrowboats Tel: 01869 340348	■	■					■									
Goodman & Bustard Tel: 01869 331508	■	■	■			■		■		■			■		■	
College Cruisers Tel: 01865 54343	■	■		■			■		■	■	■		■			■

Directory

Canal Office:
British Waterways
(Oxford and Grand Union Canals)
The Stop House
Braunston
Northamptonshire NN11 7JQ
Tel: 01788 890666

Southern Region Office:
British Waterways
Brindley House
Corner Hall
Lawn Lane
Hemel Hempstead
Hertfordshire HP3 9YT
Tel: 01442 235400

Headquarters:
British Waterways
Willow Grange
Church Road
Watford
Hertfordshire WD1 3QA
Tel: 01923 226422

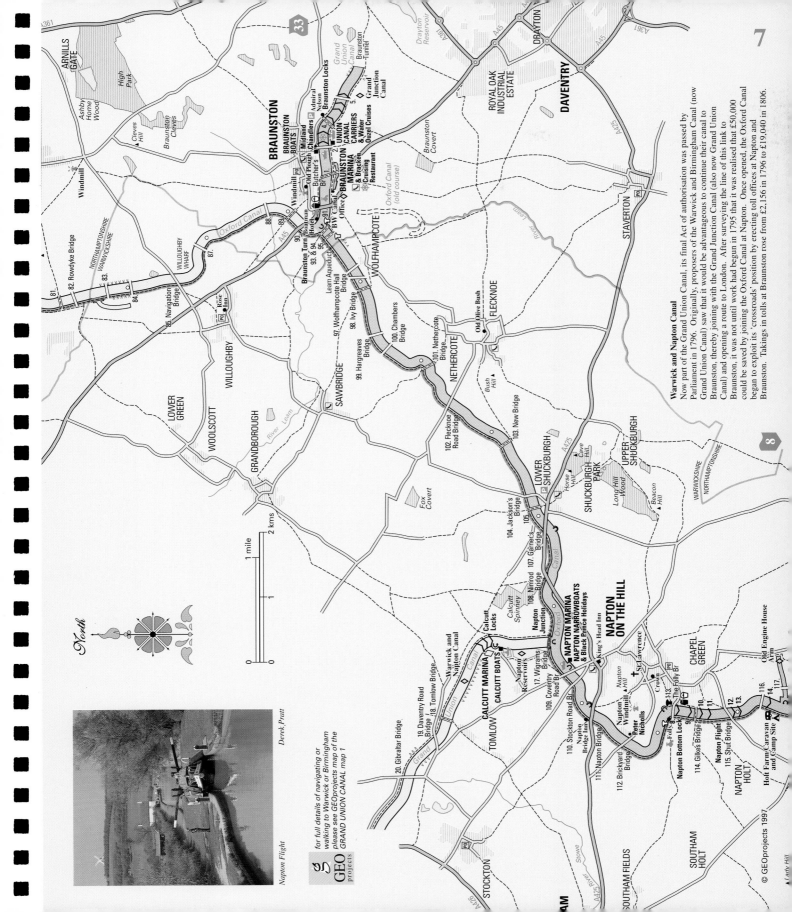

33

8

Warwick and Napton Canal

Now part of the Grand Union Canal, its final Act of authorisation was passed by Parliament in 1796. Originally, proposers of the Warwick and Birmingham Canal (now Grand Union Canal) saw that it would be advantageous to continue their canal to Braunston, thereby joining with the Grand Junction Canal (also now Grand Union Canal) and opening a route to London. After surveying the line of this link to Braunston, it was not until work had begun in 1795 that it was realised that £50,000 could be saved by joining the Oxford Canal at Napton. Once opened, the Oxford Canal began to exploit its 'crossroads' position by erecting toll offices at Napton and Braunston. Takings in tolls at Braunston rose from £2,156 in 1796 to £19,040 in 1806.

Napton Flight

Derek Pratt

for full details of navigating or walking to Warwick or Birmingham please see GEOprojects map of the GRAND UNION CANAL map 1

GEO projects

© GEOprojects 1997

North

0   1 mile
0   1   2 kms

BRAUNSTON
Admiral Nelson
Braunston Locks
Midland Chandlers
UNION CANAL CARRIERS & Water Ouzel Cruises
Grand Junction Canal
Grand Union Canal
Braunston Tunnel
Old Plough
Butcher's Br
Braunston Boats
Windmill
Boatman
Hotel
BRAUNSTON MARINA
Bracken Cruising Restaurant
BW Canal Office
Braunston Turn
Leam Aqueduct
Wolhampcote Hall Bridge
WOLFHAMPCOTE
Oxford Canal (old course)

87
88
89
90
91
93 & 94
95
97. Wolfhampcote Bridge
98. Ivy Bridge
99. Hargreaves Bridge
100. Chambers Bridge
101. Nethercote Bridge

NETHERCOTE
Old Olive Bush
FLECKNOE
Bush Hill
102. Flecknoe Road Bridge
103. New Bridge
104. Jackson's Bridge
105.
107. Garner's Bridge
108. Nimrod Bridge

LOWER SHUCKBURGH
SHUCKBURGH PARK
Cave Hill
Horse Hill
Long Hill Wood
Beacon Hill
UPPER SHUCKBURGH

WARWICKSHIRE
NORTHAMPTONSHIRE

DAVENTRY
ROYAL OAK INDUSTRIAL ESTATE
STAVERTON
Drayton Reservoir
DRAYTON

ARNILLS GATE
High Park
Ashby Home Wood
Cleves Hill
Braunston Cleves
Windmill
NORTHAMPTONSHIRE
WARWICKSHIRE
81
82. Rowdyke Bridge
83
84
85. Navigation Bridge
Oxford Canal
WILLOUGHBY WHARF
Rose Inn
LOWER GREEN
WILLOUGHBY
WOOLSCOTT
GRANDBOROUGH
River Leam
Fox Covert

SAWBRIDGE

Calcutt Locks
Calcutt Spinney
CALCUTT MARINA
CALCUTT BOATS
Warwick and Napton Canal
Napton Reservoir
TOMLOW
18. Tomlow Bridge
19. Daventry Road Bridge
20. Gibraltar Bridge
Grand Union Canal
STOCKTON
SOUTHAM FIELDS
STOCKTON HOLT
Stowe

Napton Junction
Oxford Canal
NAPTON MARINA
NAPTON NARROWBOATS & Black Prince Holidays
17. Wigrams Bridge
109. Coventry Road Br
110. Stockton Road Br
King's Head Inn
NAPTON ON THE HILL
St Lawrence
Napton Windmill
Peter Nicholls
Napton Bridge Inn
111. Napton Bridge
112. Brickyard Bridge
Napton Bottom Lock
114. Gibkes Bridge
115. Shuf Bridge
Napton Flight
The Folly Br
CHAPEL GREEN
Crow's
113
Folly Br
116
117
Old Engine House
Holt Farm Caravan and Camp Site
NAPTON HOLT
SOUTHAM HOLT
Napton Hill

A361 A45 A425 A361

Old Engine House Arm

This 900 yard (823 metre) long arm stretching eastwards off the Oxford Canal between locks 14 and 15 on the Napton Flight was built with a steam pumping engine at its eastern end. The length of this arm is explained by the passing of an Act of Parliament in 1786 enabling the Oxford Canal Company to utilize water found within 1000 yards (914 metres) of the canal. The purpose of the pump was to raise water into a brick channel which discharged into the Summit Pound near Marston Doles.

The pumping station ceased operation in 1811 with the completion of Boddington Reservoir.

Meandering Canal

The distinguished canal engineer James Brindley (1716-1772), chief engineer of the Oxford Canal, is famous for designing canals which followed the contours of the terrain: the Oxford Canal is entirely typical. The most extravagant curves occur around Wormleighton on the Summit Pound where a 3 mile (4.5 km) stretch loops back to 950 yards (868 metres) from its starting point.

Fenny Compton Tunnel

In contrast to the sweeping meanders of the canal around Wormleighton, the Oxford Canal is entrenched in a long, straight cutting south of Fenny Marina. Still known, rather anomalously, as Fenny Compton Tunnel, this steep sided cutting was originally a brick-built tunnel of 1138 yards (1040 metres) long, 12 feet (3.66 metres) high and 9 feet (2.75 metres) wide. It was decided that the tunnel should be opened up as it caused delays to traders using the canal. So the southern and northern halves of Fenny Compton Tunnel were removed in 1865 and 1866 respectively, following the purchase of the land over the tunnel from Christ Church, Oxford. To accommodate the feeder canal from Wormleighton Reservoir which crossed the southern half of the tunnel, an open topped, wrought iron channel was placed over the cutting; this has since been removed.

Boddington Reservoir

Like all canals, the Oxford Canal is dependent upon a regular, reliable source of water. To counteract water shortages on the canal's summit level between Napton Top and Claydon Top Locks the canal was fed by water from Clattercote Reservoir, approximately 1 mile (1.5 km) south-west of Claydon, and Byfield Reservoir, around 3 miles (4.5 km) north-east of Claydon. This soon proved to be inadequate and Wormleighton Reservoir was constructed. In turn a pumping station was added, built near Marston Doles, to lift water to the highest section of the canal. With boat traffic rapidly increasing in the early years of the nineteenth century, especially since the opening of the Warwick and Napton Canal, there was great demand for even more water. So the Warwick and Napton Canal Company funded the construction of Boddington Reservoir, built between 1805 and 1811. It has since been enlarged twice and the feeder channel enters the canal just west of Hay Bridge.

Byfield Pool, formerly Byfield Reservoir, no longer supplies water to the Oxford Canal and has become an attractive haven for waterfowl.

Boddington Reservoir is now home to Banbury Sailing Club, provides excellent fishing for Roach, Carp and Tench and makes for a pleasant circular walk of about 1 mile (1.5 km).

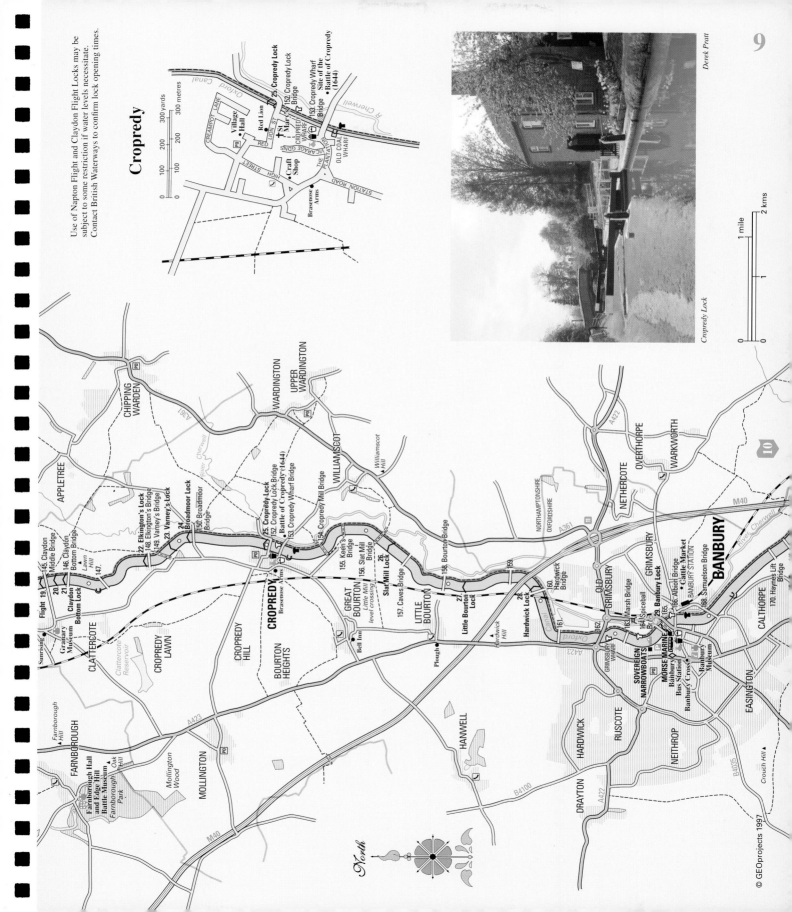

Use of Napton Flight and Claydon Flight Locks may be subject to some restriction if water levels necessitate. Contact British Waterways to confirm lock opening times.

Cropredy

Cropredy Lock

Derek Pratt

© GEOprojects 1997

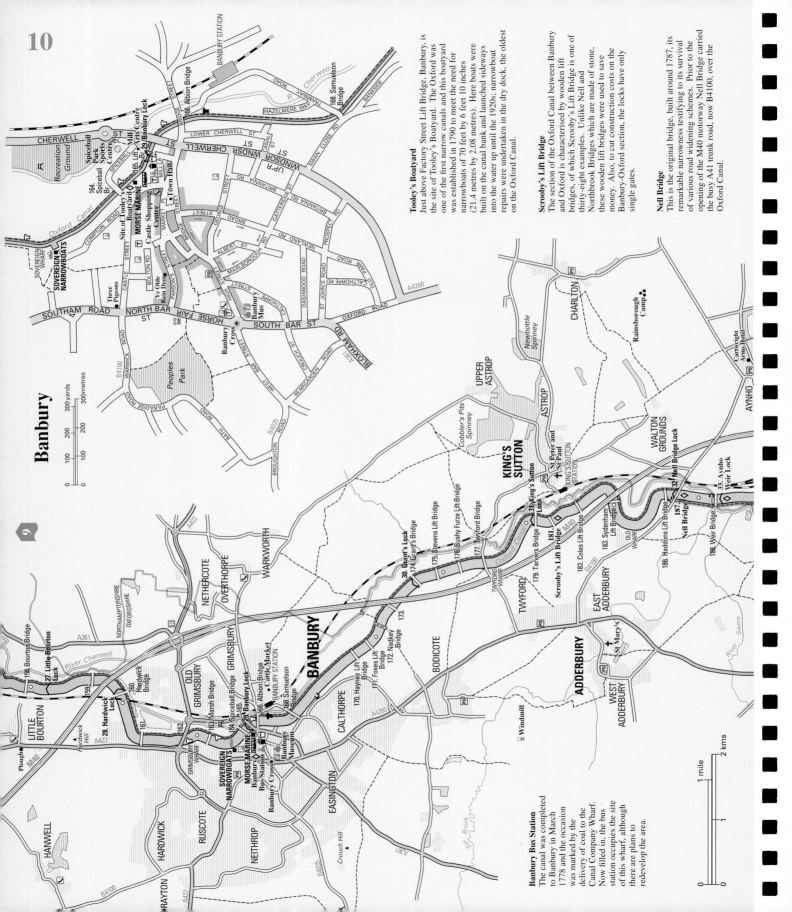

Banbury

Tooley's Boatyard

Just above Factory Street Lift Bridge, Banbury, is the site of Tooley's Boatyard. The Oxford was one of the first narrow canals and this boatyard was established in 1790 to meet the need for narrowboats of 70 feet by 6 feet 10 inches (21.4 metres by 2.08 metres). Here boats were built on the canal bank and launched sideways into the water up until the 1920s; narrowboat repairs were undertaken in the dry dock, the oldest on the Oxford Canal.

Scrooby's Lift Bridge

The section of the Oxford Canal between Banbury and Oxford is characterised by wooden lift bridges, of which Scrooby's Lift Bridge is one of thirty-eight examples. Unlike Nell and Northbrook Bridges which are made of stone, these wooden lift bridges were used to save money. Also, to cut construction costs on the Banbury-Oxford section, the locks have only single gates.

Nell Bridge

This is the original bridge, built around 1787, its remarkable narrowness testifying to its survival of various road widening schemes. Prior to the opening of the M40 motorway Nell Bridge carried the busy A41 trunk road, now B4100, over the Oxford Canal.

Banbury Bus Station

The canal was completed to Banbury in March 1778 and the occasion was marked by the delivery of coal to the Canal Company Wharf. Now filled in, the bus station occupies the site of this wharf, although there are plans to redevelop the area.

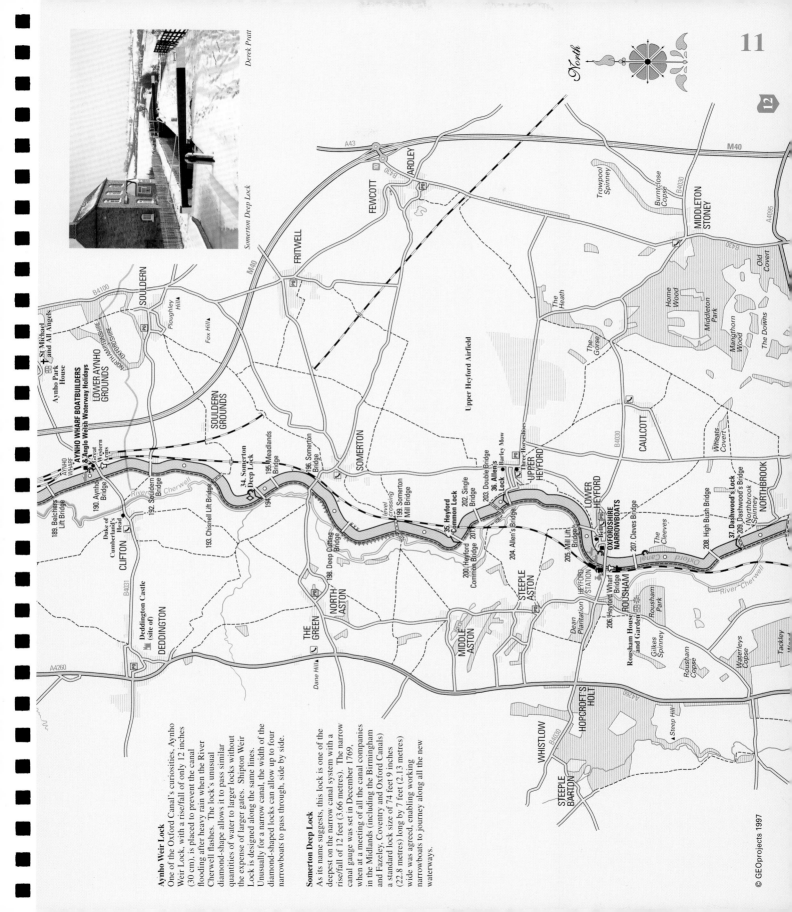

Derek Pratt

Somerton Deep Lock

North

Aynho Weir Lock

One of the Oxford Canal's curiosities, Aynho Weir Lock, with a rise/fall of only 12 inches (30 cm), is placed to prevent the canal flooding after heavy rain when the River Cherwell flashes. The lock's unusual diamond-shape allows it to pass similar quantities of water to larger locks without the expense of larger gates. Shipton Weir Lock is designed along the same lines.
Unusually for a narrow canal, the width of the diamond-shaped locks can allow up to four narrowboats to pass through, side by side.

Somerton Deep Lock

As its name suggests, this lock is one of the deepest on the narrow canal system with a rise/fall of 12 feet (3.66 metres). The narrow canal gauge was set in December 1769, when at a meeting of all the canal companies in the Midlands (including the Birmingham and Fazeley, Coventry and Oxford Canals) a standard lock size of 74 feet 9 inches (22.8 metres) long by 7 feet (2.13 metres) wide was agreed, enabling working narrowboats to journey along all the new waterways.

© GEOprojects 1997

Map labels

FEWCOTT
ARDLEY
M40
MIDDLETON STONEY
Trowpool Spinney
Burntclose Copse
Old Covert
The Downs
Home Wood
Middleton Park
Mangthorn Wood
The Heath
The Gorse
Wheats Covert
CAULCOTT
Upper Heyford Airfield
SOULDERN
Ploughley Hill ▲
Fox Hill ▲
St Michael and All Angels
Aynho Park House
LOWER AYNHO GROUNDS
SOULDERN GROUNDS
SOMERTON
Three Horseshoes
Barley Mow
UPPER HEYFORD
LOWER HEYFORD
NORTHBROOK
Northbrook Spinney
AYNHO WHARF BOATBUILDERS & Anglo Welsh Waterway Holidays
Great Western Arms
AYNHO WHARF
Duke of Cumberland's Head
189. Belchers Lift Bridge
190. Aynho Bridge
192. Souldern Bridge
193. Chisnell Lift Bridge
194.
195. Meadlands Bridge
196. Somerton Bridge
34. Somerton Deep Lock
198. Deep Cutting Bridge
199. Somerton Mill Bridge
200. Heyford Common Bridge
201.
35. Heyford Common Lock
202. Single Bridge
203. Double Bridge
36. Allen's Lock
204. Allen's Bridge
205. Mill Lift Bridge
206. Heyford Wharf Bridge
207. Cleves Bridge
208. High Bush Bridge
37. Dashwood's Lock
209. Dashwood's Bridge
level crossing
CLIFTON
Deddington Castle (site of)
DEDDINGTON
NORTH ASTON
THE GREEN
Dane Hill ▲
MIDDLE ASTON
STEEPLE ASTON
Dean Plantation
HEYFORD STATION
OXFORDSHIRE NARROWBOATS
ROUSHAM
Rousham House and Garden
Gilkes Spinney
Rousham Park
Rousham Copse
The Cleeves
Waterleys Copse
Tackley Wood
HOPCROFT'S HOLT
Steep Hill ▲
WHISTLOW
STEEPLE BARTON
River Cherwell
Oxford Canal
B4100
A43
B430
B4030
A4095
A4260
B4031
A4260
M40
NORTHAMPTONSHIRE
OXFORDSHIRE
FRITWELL

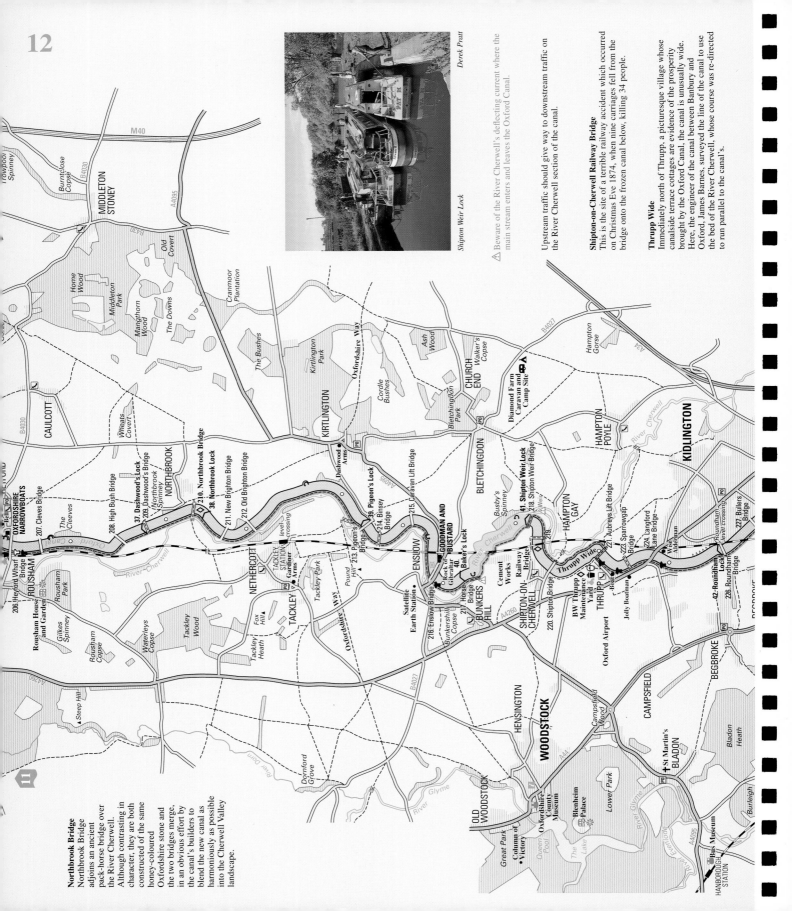

Shipton Weir Lock

Derek Pratt

△ Beware of the River Cherwell's deflecting current where the main stream enters and leaves the Oxford Canal.

Upstream traffic should give way to downstream traffic on the River Cherwell section of the canal.

Shipton-on-Cherwell Railway Bridge
This is the site of a terrible railway accident which occurred on Christmas Eve 1874, when nine carriages fell from the bridge onto the frozen canal below, killing 34 people.

Thrupp Wide
Immediately north of Thrupp, a picturesque village whose canalside terrace cottages are evidence of the prosperity brought by the Oxford Canal, the canal is unusually wide. Here, the engineer of the canal between Banbury and Oxford, James Barnes, surveyed the line of the canal to use the bed of the River Cherwell, whose course was re-directed to run parallel to the canal's.

Northbrook Bridge
Northbrook Bridge adjoins an ancient pack-horse bridge over the River Cherwell. Although contrasting in character, they are both constructed of the same honey-coloured Oxfordshire stone and the two bridges merge, in an obvious effort by the canal's builders to blend the new canal as harmoniously as possible into the Cherwell Valley landscape.

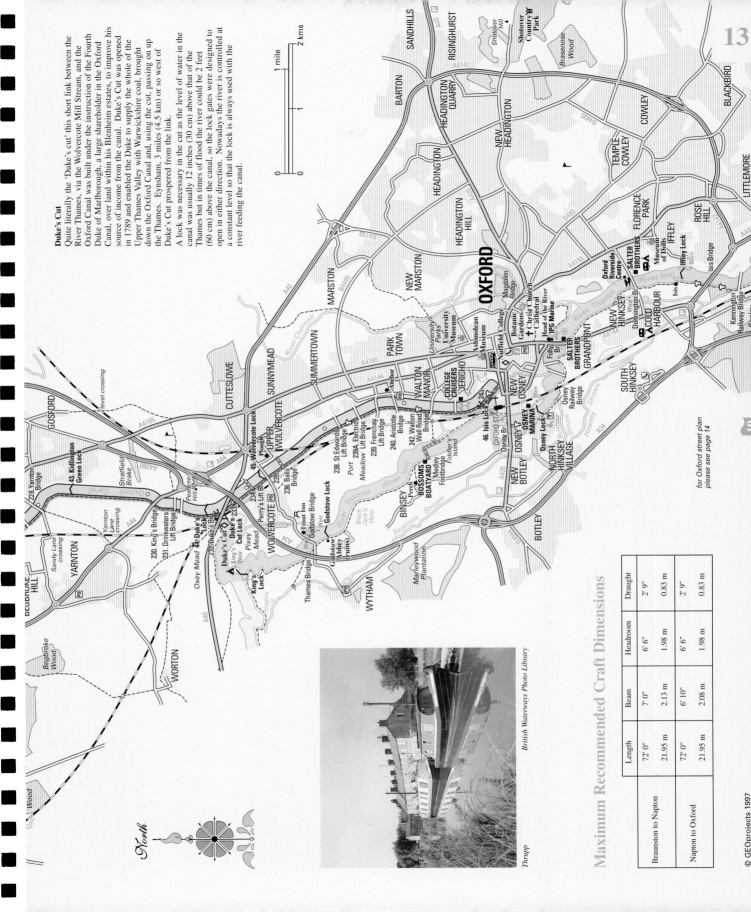

Duke's Cut

Quite literally the 'Duke's cut' this short link between the River Thames, via the Wolvercote Mill Stream, and the Oxford Canal was built under the instruction of the Fourth Duke of Marlborough, a large shareholder in the Oxford Canal, over land within his Blenheim estates, to improve his source of income from the canal. Duke's Cut was opened in 1789 and enabled the Duke to supply the whole of the Upper Thames Valley with Warwickshire coal, brought down the Oxford Canal and, using the cut, passing on up the Thames. Eynsham, 3 miles (4.5 km) or so west of Duke's Cut prospered from the link.

A lock was necessary in the cut as the level of water in the canal was usually 12 inches (30 cm) above that of the Thames but in times of flood the river could be 2 feet (60 cm) above the canal, so the lock gates were designed to open in either direction. Nowadays the river is controlled at a constant level so that the lock is always used with the river feeding the canal.

North

British Waterways Photo Library

Thrupp

Maximum Recommended Craft Dimensions

	Length		Beam		Headroom		Draught	
Braunston to Napton	72' 0"	21.95 m	7' 0"	2.13 m	6' 6"	1.98 m	2' 9"	0.83 m
Napton to Oxford	72' 0"	21.95 m	6' 10"	2.08 m	6' 6"	1.98 m	2' 9"	0.83 m

for Oxford street plan please see page 14

© GEOprojects 1997

14

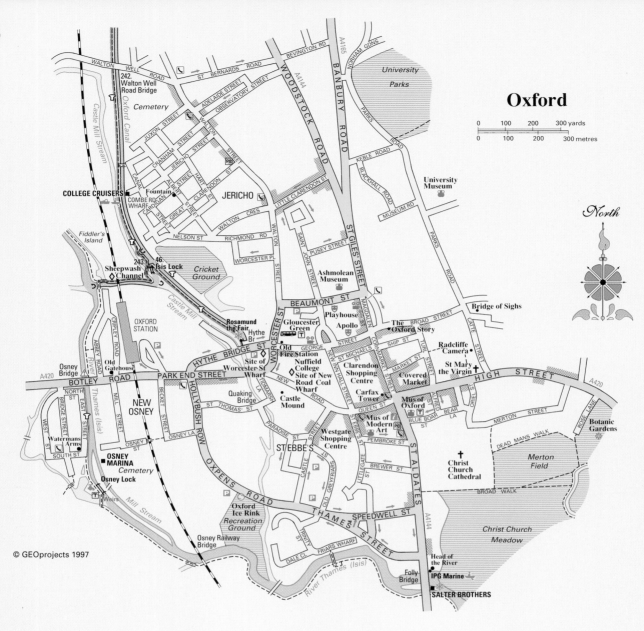

Oxford

0   100   200   300 yards
0   100   200   300 metres

North

Labels on map: WALTON WELL ROAD · 242. Walton Well Road Bridge · Cemetery · ST BERNARDS ROAD · BEVINGTON RD · A4165 · NORHAM GDNS · University Parks · Oxford Canal · Castle Mill Stream · ADELAIDE STREET · OBSERVATORY STREET · WOODSTOCK ROAD · BANBURY ROAD · JUXON STREET · CRANHAM STREET · JERICHO STREET · HART STREET · CLARENDON STREET · KEBLE ROAD · BLACKHALL ROAD · MUSEUM RD · University Museum · COLLEGE CRUISERS · Fountain · COMBE RD · CANAL ST · GREAT CLARENDON ST · JERICHO · LITTLE CLARENDON ST · WALTON CRES · RICHMOND RD · NELSON ST · WORCESTER PL · ST JOHN STREET · PUSEY STREET · ST GILES STREET · PARKS ROAD · Fiddler's Island · 243. · 46. Isis Lock · Sheepwash Channel · Cricket Ground · Castle Mill Stream · Ashmolean Museum · BEAUMONT ST · MAGDALEN ST · BROAD STREET · Bridge of Sighs · Radcliffe Camera · St Mary the Virgin · OXFORD STATION · CRIPLEY ROAD · Rosamund the Fair · Hythe Br · Gloucester Green · Playhouse · Apollo · The Oxford Story · SHIP ST · TURL STREET · CATTE STREET · Osney Bridge · Old Gatehouse · ABBEY ROAD · HYTHE BRIDGE ST · WORCESTER ST · Site of Worcester St Wharf · Old Fire Station · Nuffield College · Site of New Road Coal Wharf · Clarendon Shopping Centre · Covered Market · Carfax Tower · MARKET ST · CORNMARKET ST · A420 · Osney Bridge · BOTLEY ROAD · PARK END STREET · NORTH ST · EAST ST · BRIDGE STREET · WEST ST · SOUTH ST · Watermans Arms · NEW OSNEY · MILL STREET · BECKET ST · HOLLYBUSH ROW · ST THOMAS' ST · Quaking Bridge · Castle Mound · NEW ROAD · QUEEN ST · Mus of Oxford · BEAR LA · BLUE BOAR · ALFRED ST · HIGH STREET · MERTON STREET · ROSE LANE · Botanic Gardens · OSNEY MARINA · Cemetery · Osney Lock · OSNEY LA · PARADISE ST · CASTLE ST · Mus of Modern Art · Westgate Shopping Centre · ST EBBE'S · PEMBROKE ST · LITTLEGATE ST · OLD GREYFRIARS ST · BREWER ST · ST ALDATES · DEAD MANS WALK · Merton Field · Weirs · Mill Stream · OXPENS ROAD · Oxford Ice Rink · Recreation Ground · THAMES STREET · SPEEDWELL ST · TRINITY · DALE CL · FRIARS WHARF · Christ Church Cathedral · BROAD WALK · Christ Church Meadow · A4144 · Osney Railway Bridge · River Thames (Isis) · Head of the River · Folly Bridge · IPG Marine · SALTER BROTHERS · © GEOprojects 1997

Sheepwash Channel

For about six years or so Duke's Cut provided the only link between the Oxford Canal and the River Thames. Although navigable, the journey upstream of Oxford on the Thames was notoriously bad, particularly between Osney and King's Weir, and this, combined with the Oxford Canal Company's wish for its own connection with the Thames, led to the widening and dredging of Sheepwash Channel, a backwater of the river, and the construction of Isis Lock. Built in 1796, Isis Lock was capable of accommodating the larger Thames barges so that the Canal Company could trade directly onto the river from its Worcester Street and New Road Wharves.

The completion of the Birmingham and Fazeley Canal in 1789 to its junction with the Trent and Mersey Canal and the completion of the Coventry Canal a year later meant that the waterway link between Liverpool and London, via the Oxford Canal and River Thames, was complete.

Nuffield College

Nuffield College stands on the site of the original terminus of the Oxford Canal. Completed in 1789, the Worcester Street and New Road Wharves beyond Hythe Bridge Street were officially opened on New Year's Day 1790 when celebrations were held to welcome the first 200 tons of cargo into the centre of Oxford. Within weeks of coal arriving at the basin, fuel prices dropped dramatically and gradually the canal brought economic prosperity to the city.

The land around the two wharves was sold by the Canal Company to Lord Nuffield in 1936. Work on building Nuffield College commenced in 1949.

Near Duke's Cut   British Waterways Photo Library

River Thames

OXFORD CANAL   GRAND UNION CANAL

RIVER THAMES

Comprising the 99 mile (159 km) stretch of the Thames Ring between Oxford and Brentford, the River Thames also forms the southern portion of the London Ring from Brentford to Limehouse along 11 miles (17.5 km) of tidal water.

Passing through Duke's Cut with its shallow lock and then along the Wolvercote Mill Stream and King's Weirstream the Thames proper is reached at King's Lock, the most northerly point of this great river's winding course. Each of the 34 locks between here and Teddington has a lock-keeper and when compared to the narrow locks of the Oxford Canal, built to accommodate narrowboats of 72' by 7', the lock dimensions are enormous. They range in size from Godstow Lock at 110' (33.52 metres) by 16'3" (4.95 metres) to the cavernous Teddington Barge Lock at 650' (198.12 metres) by 24'10" (7.56 metres).

Transitting Isis Lock near the terminus of the Oxford Canal and passing along Sheepwash Channel leads to the canal's second junction with the Thames at a waterway crossroads known as Four Rivers. Turning downstream, Osney Bridge is the first encountered and is the lowest on the river with a headroom of 7'6" (2.28 metres).

History

The Thames has been used for transportation from prehistoric times and the right to navigation on the river is recognised in Clause 23 of the Magna Carta, signed by King John at Runnymede in 1215. However, weirs built across the river to provide water power for millers and to benefit fisheries (fish were caught in the weir pool), acted as obstacles to navigation. Flash weirs were developed where a temporary opening allowed boats to shoot the rapids going downstream and be hauled by horse upstream. These were a feature on the river from the 13th century through to the 1880s and, until the arrival of pound locks, were a continuous source of conflict between boats wanting to pass through the weirs and millers who experienced a reduction in water power each time they did so. The last remaining example, Hart's Weir, located above Oxford at Burcot on the Upper Thames, was removed in 1937. During the 1630s the first pound locks were introduced at Iffley, Sandford and Abingdon by the Oxford-Burcot Commissioners, a body established to improve navigation to Oxford. The significance of the river as a trading highway increased with the opening of the Thames and Severn Canal (1789), the Oxford Canal (1790) and the Kennet and Avon Canal (1810). From 1751 Thames Commissioners were appointed along the length of the navigable river to Lechlade establishing a towing path, building more pound locks and generally improving the river to fulfil its major role in the country's inland waterway network. Commercial carrying on the Thames began to decline after the opening of the Great Western Railway to Reading (1840) and to Bristol (1841). In 1858 Salter's established their pioneering passenger services and around 1900 were operating two trips a day each way between Oxford and Kingston, the journey taking 2½ days. The Thames was increasingly exploited for pleasure use from mid-Victorian times with steam-boats, punts, skiffs and rowing becoming very popular. At the turn of the century Boulter's Lock, Maidenhead, was the busiest on the river being noted for its fashionable punting parties. The trend towards cruiser hiring/owning began in the 1920s. The Environment Agency is now the navigation authority for the freshwater Thames while jurisdiction of the river below Teddington has rested with the Port of London Authority since its formation in 1908.

Look out for

◊ **Sandford Lock** This is the deepest lock on the river above Teddington with a rise/fall of 8'10" (2.69 metres).

◊ **Goring Gap** The typically broad, shallow valley of the Thames narrows at Goring where the river passes between the chalk ridges of the Chilterns and the Berkshire Downs.

◊ **Mapledurham Mill** This is the only working flour mill left on the Thames, originally 15th century; the ground wholewheat flour is on sale in the mill shop.

◊ **Henley Reach** Henley Reach is the location of the famous Henley Royal Regatta course from Temple Island to just downstream of Henley Bridge.

◊ **Maidenhead Railway Bridge** Built by Brunel in 1839, this bridge has the widest brick-built spans in the world at 128' (39 metres).

◊ **London Stone** From 1285 the London Stone, located upstream of Staines Bridge, marked the upstream limit of the city of London's jurisdiction on the Thames until the establishment of the Thames Conservancy in 1857.

◊ **Teddington Locks** Teddington has the longest weir with an average daily discharge of 1,535,000,000 gallons of water and the largest locking system on the River Thames. They mark the transition between the freshwater and tidal Thames.

Maximum Craft Dimensions

The Thames is normally navigable by vessels of the following approximate draughts:

Above Oxford	3' 0"	(0.91 metres)
Oxford to Reading	4' 0"	(1.21 metres)
Reading to Windsor	4' 6"	(1.37 metres)
Windsor to Staines	5' 6"	(1.67 metres)
Staines to Teddington	6' 6"	(2.01 metres)

River Thames, near Marlow   *Derek Pratt*

Marina and Boatyard Facilities

Oxford to Egham

	Long-term mooring	Temporary/overnight mooring	Slipway	Water	Refuse disposal	Elsan disposal	Pump out	Electricity points	Bottled gas	Diesel	Boat/engine repairs	Cranage	Hardstanding	Parts and equipment	Boat sales	Chandlery/shop
Bossoms Boatyard Tel: 01865 247780	■	■	■	■	■		■	■	■		■	■	■	■	■	
Osney Marina Tel: 01865 241348	■	■	■	■		■	■			■			■		■	
Salter Brothers (Folly Br) Tel: 01865 243421			■	■							■				■	
Salter Brothers (Don'ton Br) Tel: (as above)				■	■				■							
Abingdon Boat Centre Tel: 01235 521125	■	■	■	■			■	■	■	■			■	■		
Red Line Cruisers Tel: 01235 535878	■	■	■	■		■	■		■	■				■		
Benson Pleasure Craft Tel: 01491 838304	■	■	■	■			■	■	■	■	■		■			
Maidline Cruisers Tel: 01491 836088			■	■					■			■				
Sheridan UK Marine Tel: 01491 652085	■	■	■	■				■	■	■	■		■	■	■	
Bridge Boats Tel: 0118 959 0346	■	■	■	■				■	■	■						
Caversham Boat Services Tel: 0118 957 4323	■		■	■		■	■		■				■	■		
Better Boating Tel: 0118 947 9536	■		■	■	■	■	■	■	■		■		■			
Thames and Kennet Marina Tel: 0118 948 2911			■	■		■	■	■	■	■		■		■	■	
Bushnell's Boatyard Tel: 0118 940 2161	■										■	■	■			
Val Wyatt Marine Tel: 0118 940 3211	■	■	■	■			■	■	■	■	■		■	■	■	
Peter Freebody Tel: 01628 824382	■	■	■	■	■			■	■	■	■			■	■	
Harleyford Marina Tel: 01628 471361	■	■	■	■	■	■	■	■	■		■		■	■	■	
Wootten's Boatyard Tel: 01628 484244	■	■	■	■		■	■			■			■	■		
Bourne End Marina Tel: 01628 522813	■	■	■	■	■	■	■	■	■	■	■		■	■	■	■
D B Marine Tel: 01628 526032	■										■					
Bray Marina Tel: 01628 23654	■	■	■	■		■	■	■	■	■	■		■	■	■	■
Windsor Marina Tel: 01753 853911	■	■	■	■	■	■	■	■	■	■			■	■	■	
Racecourse Yacht Basin Tel: 01753 851501	■	■	■	■		■			■	■	■		■	■	■	■
Tom Jones Boatbuilders Tel: 01753 860699	■										■	■	■			
Kris Cruisers Tel: 01753 543930		■		■	■	■	■		■	■	■					
Wraysbury Boathouse Tel: 01784 482569	■	■	■						■	■	■		■	■	■	■
Nicholes Boatyard Tel: 01784 432342	■		■	■	■				■	■	■				■	■

The Environment Agency has four navigation inspection offices along the River Thames

Environment Agency
Navigation Inspector
(Cricklade Bridge to tail of Benson Lock Cut)
Osney Lock
Bridge Street
Oxford
Oxfordshire OX2 0AX
Tel: 01865 721271

Environment Agency
District Navigation Inspector
(Tail of Benson Lock Cut to
tail of Hurley Lower Lock Cut)
Kings Meadow House
Kings Meadow Road
Reading
Berkshire RG1 8BP
Tel: 0118 953 5533

Environment Agency
Navigation Inspector
(Hurley Weir Stream to Penton Hook Lock)
Boulter's Lock
Raymead Road
Maidenhead
Berkshire SL6 8PE
Tel: 01628 22491

Environment Agency
Navigation Inspector
(Penton Hook Lower Lock Cut to
Teddington)
Riverside Works
Fordbridge Road
Sunbury
Surrey TW16 6AP
Tel: 01932 781946

Further information on boat user
facilities can be obtained from:
The Thames Boating Trade Association
No 1 The Moorings
Straight Road
Old Windsor
Berkshire
Tel: 01753 860393

Further information on cruiser hire
can be obtained from:
Thames Hire Cruiser Association
19 Acre End Street
Eynsham
Witney
Oxfordshire OX8 1PE
Tel: 01865 880107

Further information on passenger boat trips
can be obtained from:
The Upper Thames Passenger Boat
Association
PO Box 679
Windsor
Berkshire SL4 5JU
Tel: 01344 890351
Tel: 01753 851900 (message service)

For information and membership details
of the River Thames Society contact:
The Administrator
Side House
Middle Assendon
Henley-on-Thames
Oxfordshire RG9 6AP
Tel: 01491 571476

Directory

Navigation Authorities

Tidal Thames
The Port of London Authority is the
navigation authority below Teddington

Port of London Authority
Devon House
58-60 St Katharine's Way
London E1 9LB
Tel: 0171 265 2656

Non-tidal Thames
The Environment Agency is the navigation
authority above Teddington

Thames Region Office
Environment Agency
Kings Meadow House
Kings Meadow Road
Reading
Berkshire RG1 8BP
Tel: 0118 953 5533

Marina and Boatyard Facilities
Staines to Teddington

Name / Tel	Long-term mooring	Temporary/overnight mooring	Slipway	Water	Refuse disposal	Elsan disposal	Pump out	Electricity points	Bottled gas	Diesel	Boat/engine repairs	Cranage	Hardstanding	Parts and equipment	Boat sales	Chandlery/shop
Aquamarine Boats — Tel: 01753 543930		■			■	■				■						■
Tecmarine — Tel: 01784 452093	■			■	■			■	■	■	■	■	■	■	■	■
Penton Hook Marina — Tel: 01932 568681	■	■	■	■	■	■	■	■	■	■	■	■	■	■	■	■
M Dennett Boatbuilders — Tel: 01932 563448		■									■		■			
Harris Boatbuilders — Tel: 01932 563111	■		■	■	■	■	■		■	■	■		■			■
Chertsey Meads Marine — Tel: 01932 564699		■	■	■	■		■		■	■		■				
Nauticalia — Tel: 01932 254844	■		■							■		■		■		■
Eyot House — Tel: 01932 848586	■		■					■		■						
Gibbs Chandlery — Tel: 01932 232145	■		■	■						■				■		■
Bridge Marine — Tel: 01932 245126		■	■							■	■	■				■
Walton Marina — Tel: 01932 226266	■									■	■		■			
Shepperton Marina — Tel: 01932 243722	■	■	■	■	■	■	■	■	■	■	■	■	■	■	■	■
Vjera Line Cruises — Tel: 01932 252520	■									■						
G Wilson and Sons — Tel: 01932 782067	■		■							■						
Port Hampton — Tel: 0181 979 8116	■					■						■	■			
Thames Voyages — Tel: 0181 941 2676	■		■	■	■					■			■	■		
Hucks — Tel: 0181 979 2135	■		■				■	■		■						
T W Allen and Son — Tel: 0181 979 1997	■	■						■		■			■	■		
Tagg's Boatyard — Tel: 0181 398 2119	■	■		■	■			■		■			■	■		
Ferryline Cruisers — Tel: 0181 398 0271		■		■	■	■	■			■	■					
Thames Ditton Marina — Tel: 0181 398 6159	■	■	■	■			■	■		■	■		■	■		■
Hart's Boatyard — Tel: 0181 399 4009	■	■								■						
Suntest Marine/Teddington Harbour — Tel: 0181 977 9978	■	■	■					■	■	■			■	■		■
Tough Brothers — Tel: 0181 977 4494	■	■	■	■			■	■		■		■	■		■	■

Thames Locks

Northmoor Lock	Tel: 01865 862923
Pinkhill Lock	Tel: 01865 881452
Eynsham Lock	Tel: 01865 881324
King's Lock	Tel: 01865 53403
Godstow Lock	Tel: 01865 54784
Osney Lock	Tel: 01865 247050
Iffley Lock	Tel: 01865 777277
Sandford Lock	Tel: 01865 775889
Abingdon Lock	Tel: 01235 523044
Culham Lock	Tel: 01235 522061
Clifton Lock	Tel: 01865 407821
Day's Lock	Tel: 01865 407768
Benson Lock	Tel: 01491 835255
Cleeve Lock	Tel: 01491 872608
Goring Lock	Tel: 01491 872687
Whitchurch Lock	Tel: 0118 984 2448
Mapledurham Lock	Tel: 0118 941 7776
Caversham Lock	Tel: 0118 957 5764
Sonning Lock	Tel: 0118 969 3992
Shiplake Lock	Tel: 0118 940 3350
Marsh Lock	Tel: 01491 572992
Hambleden Lock	Tel: 01491 571269
Hurley Lock	Tel: 01628 824334
Temple Lock	Tel: 01628 824333
Marlow Lock	Tel: 01628 482867
Cookham Lock	Tel: 01628 520752
Boulter's Lock	Tel: 01628 24205
Bray Lock	Tel: 01628 21650
Boveney Lock	Tel: 01753 862764
Romney Lock	Tel: 01753 860296
Old Windsor Lock	Tel: 01753 861822
Bell Weir Lock	Tel: 01784 432333
Penton Hook Lock	Tel: 01784 452657
Chertsey Lock	Tel: 01932 562208
Shepperton Lock	Tel: 01932 221840
Sunbury Locks	Tel: 01932 782089
Molesey Lock	Tel: 0181 979 4482
Teddington Locks	Tel: 0181 940 8723

Commonwealth Air Forces Memorial, Runnymede   *Derek Pratt*

Locks are manned during the following hours:

April	09.00 - 17.30	
May	09.00 - 18.30	
June to August	09.00 - 19.00	
September	09.00 - 18.00	(09.00 - 18.30 Sat and Sun)
October	09.00 - 17.00	
November to March	09.15 - 16.00	(09.00 - 17.30 Good Friday to Easter Monday inclusive if Easter falls in March)

Teddington lock is staffed 24 hrs a day.

Iffley Lock   Derek Pratt

Shifford Lock

Built in 1898, Shifford Lock is the youngest on the Thames. It is located at the eastern end of a tree-lined artificial cut which bypasses the loop of the river with its many tight meanders, now a peaceful backwater, near Duxford. This lock is also the most isolated lying amid the fields and meadows of rural Oxfordshire. Part of the backwater remains navigable by small craft to Duxford ford, the only surviving purpose-built ford on the river.

Tenfoot Bridge

'Tenfoot' is not a reference to the headroom under the bridge which is 12'2" (3.71 metres) but relates to a former weir, removed in 1869 when the bridge was built, which had a flash opening of 10 feet through which barges passed.

⚠ The original course of the river is only navigable by small craft from below Shifford Lock to Duxford Ford, where turning room is limited.

Swinford Bridge

Swinford Bridge was built by the Earl of Abingdon in 1777 to replace a ferry and is one of two remaining toll bridges across the river. Cars are charged 5p; emergency vehicles and post vans cross without charge.

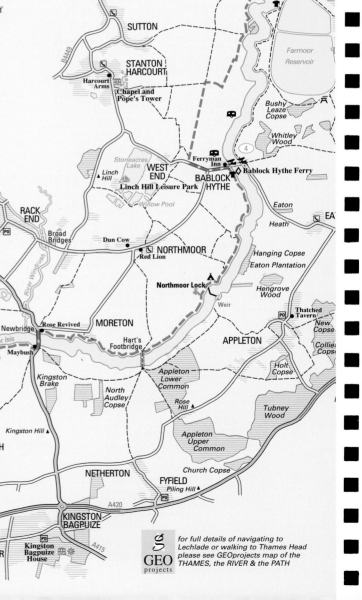

for full details of navigating to Lechlade or walking to Thames Head please see GEOprojects map of the THAMES, the RIVER & the PATH

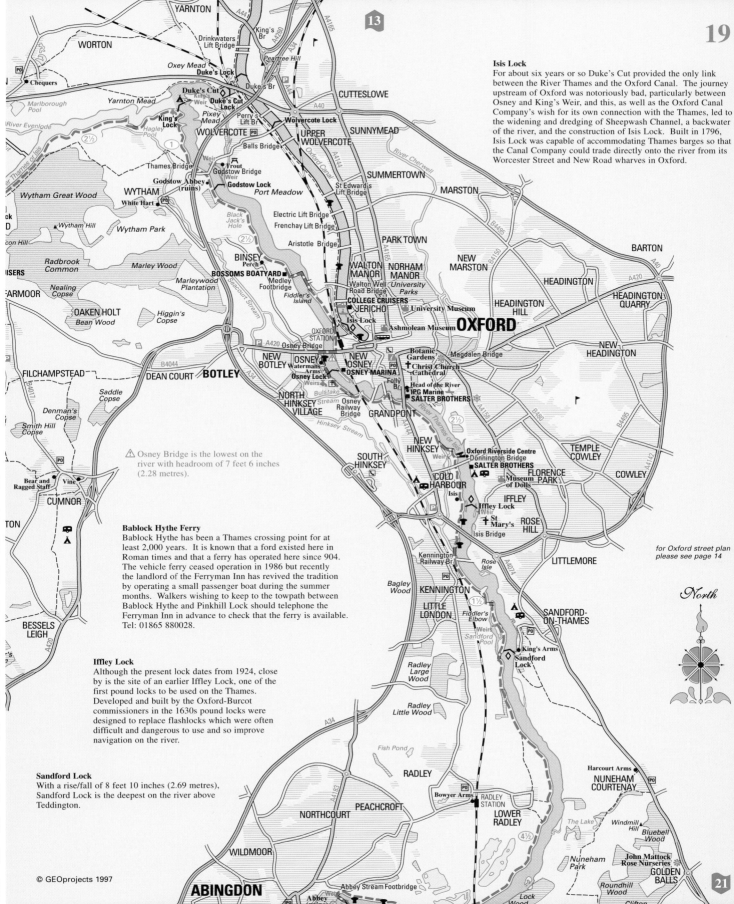

Isis Lock

For about six years or so Duke's Cut provided the only link between the River Thames and the Oxford Canal. The journey upstream of Oxford was notoriously bad, particularly between Osney and King's Weir, and this, as well as the Oxford Canal Company's wish for its own connection with the Thames, led to the widening and dredging of Sheepwash Channel, a backwater of the river, and the construction of Isis Lock. Built in 1796, Isis Lock was capable of accommodating Thames barges so that the Canal Company could trade directly onto the river from its Worcester Street and New Road wharves in Oxford.

⚠ Osney Bridge is the lowest on the river with headroom of 7 feet 6 inches (2.28 metres).

Bablock Hythe Ferry

Bablock Hythe has been a Thames crossing point for at least 2,000 years. It is known that a ford existed here in Roman times and that a ferry has operated here since 904. The vehicle ferry ceased operation in 1986 but recently the landlord of the Ferryman Inn has revived the tradition by operating a small passenger boat during the summer months. Walkers wishing to keep to the towpath between Bablock Hythe and Pinkhill Lock should telephone the Ferryman Inn in advance to check that the ferry is available. Tel: 01865 880028.

Iffley Lock

Although the present lock dates from 1924, close by is the site of an earlier Iffley Lock, one of the first pound locks to be used on the Thames. Developed and built by the Oxford-Burcot commissioners in the 1630s pound locks were designed to replace flashlocks which were often difficult and dangerous to use and so improve navigation on the river.

Sandford Lock

With a rise/fall of 8 feet 10 inches (2.69 metres), Sandford Lock is the deepest on the river above Teddington.

for Oxford street plan please see page 14

North

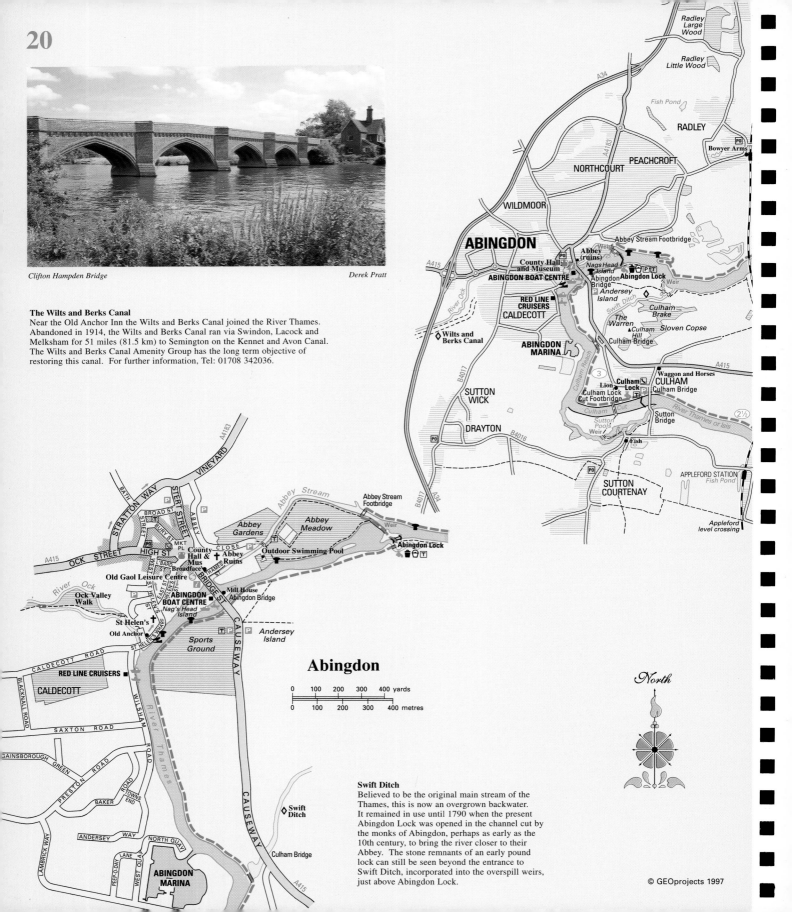

Clifton Hampden Bridge   *Derek Pratt*

The Wilts and Berks Canal

Near the Old Anchor Inn the Wilts and Berks Canal joined the River Thames.
Abandoned in 1914, the Wilts and Berks Canal ran via Swindon, Lacock and
Melksham for 51 miles (81.5 km) to Semington on the Kennet and Avon Canal.
The Wilts and Berks Canal Amenity Group has the long term objective of
restoring this canal. For further information, Tel: 01708 342036.

Abingdon

0   100   200   300   400 yards

0   100   200   300   400 metres

Swift Ditch

Believed to be the original main stream of the
Thames, this is now an overgrown backwater.
It remained in use until 1790 when the present
Abingdon Lock was opened in the channel cut by
the monks of Abingdon, perhaps as early as the
10th century, to bring the river closer to their
Abbey. The stone remnants of an early pound
lock can still be seen beyond the entrance to
Swift Ditch, incorporated into the overspill weirs,
just above Abingdon Lock.

© GEOprojects 1997

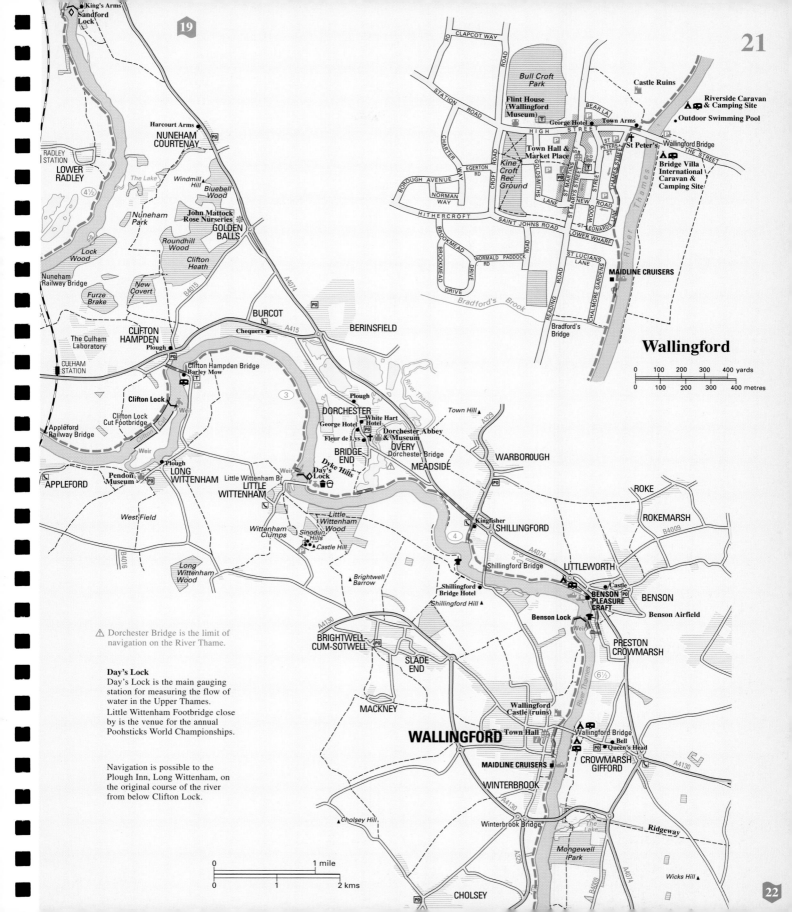

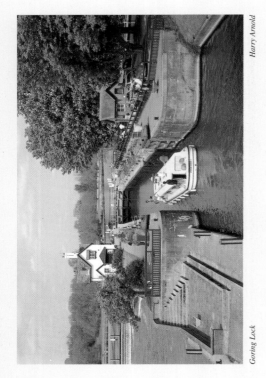

Goring Lock

Harry Arnold

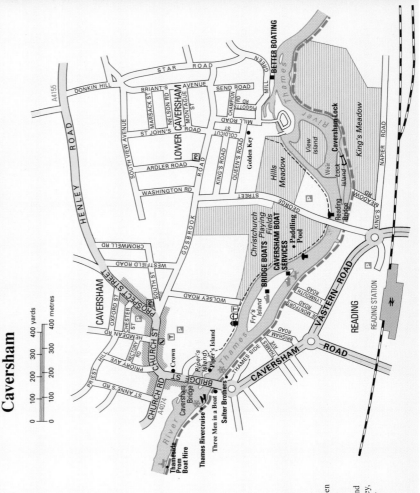

Caversham

| 0 | 100 | 200 | 300 | 400 metres |

| 0 | 100 | 200 | 300 | 400 yards |

The Goring Gap

The Thames is a lowland river with a broad, shallow valley throughout most of its course. South of Goring, though, the valley sides steepen where, during the last ice age, the Thames was glacially diverted to cut across a line of chalk hills. The Chilterns now form the north side and the Berkshire Downs the south side of the valley, known here as the Goring Gap. The Ridgeway path crosses the Thames at Goring.

21

Mapledurham Mill

Mapledurham Mill is the only working flour mill left on the Thames. After an inoperative period of thirty years this 15th century mill was fully restored to working order in 1977. It has a wooden shaft and water wheel, made of oak and elm respectively, one of only a few mills in Britain to be so. The mill's undershot wheel drives two pairs of millstones grinding a tonne of flour in six hours. The ground wholewheat flour is on sale in the mill shop.
On the opposite bank of the river is Mapledurham Lock, the first lock on the Thames to be mechanised, in 1956.

Whitchurch Bridge

Whitchurch Bridge is one of two surviving toll bridges across the river. The toll for vehicles is 8p, while pedestrians cross without charge. The present white-painted iron structure is Victorian, built in 1880.

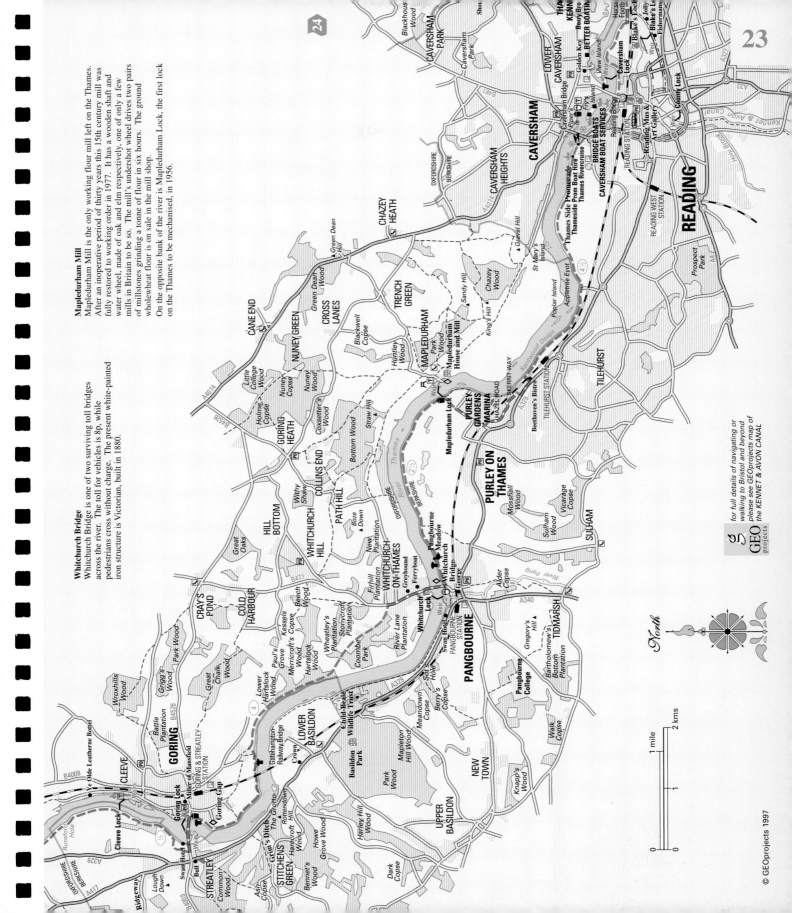

for full details of navigating or walking to Bristol and beyond please see GEOprojects map of the KENNET & AVON CANAL

GEO projects

© GEOprojects 1997

North

0   1 mile
0 1 2 kms

Henley-on-Thames

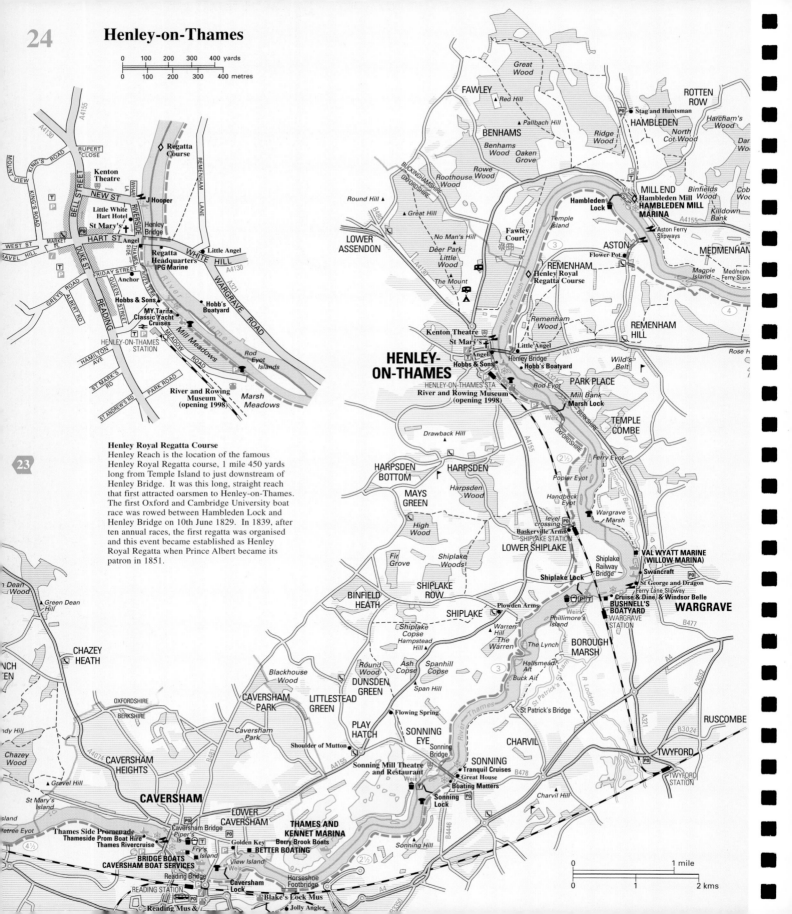

Henley Royal Regatta Course

Henley Reach is the location of the famous Henley Royal Regatta course, 1 mile 450 yards long from Temple Island to just downstream of Henley Bridge. It was this long, straight reach that first attracted oarsmen to Henley-on-Thames. The first Oxford and Cambridge University boat race was rowed between Hambleden Lock and Henley Bridge on 10th June 1829. In 1839, after ten annual races, the first regatta was organised and this event became established as Henley Royal Regatta when Prince Albert became its patron in 1851.

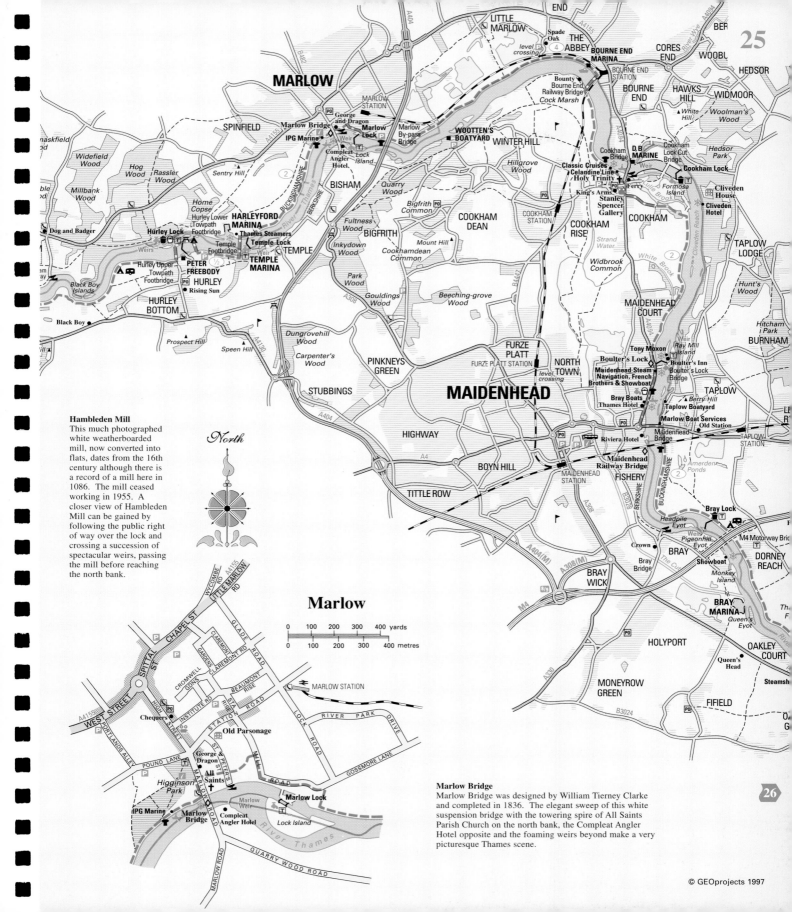

Hambleden Mill
This much photographed white weatherboarded mill, now converted into flats, dates from the 16th century although there is a record of a mill here in 1086. The mill ceased working in 1955. A closer view of Hambleden Mill can be gained by following the public right of way over the lock and crossing a succession of spectacular weirs, passing the mill before reaching the north bank.

Marlow

0 100 200 300 400 yards
0 100 200 300 400 metres

Marlow Bridge
Marlow Bridge was designed by William Tierney Clarke and completed in 1836. The elegant sweep of this white suspension bridge with the towering spire of All Saints Parish Church on the north bank, the Compleat Angler Hotel opposite and the foaming weirs beyond make a very picturesque Thames scene.

© GEOprojects 1997

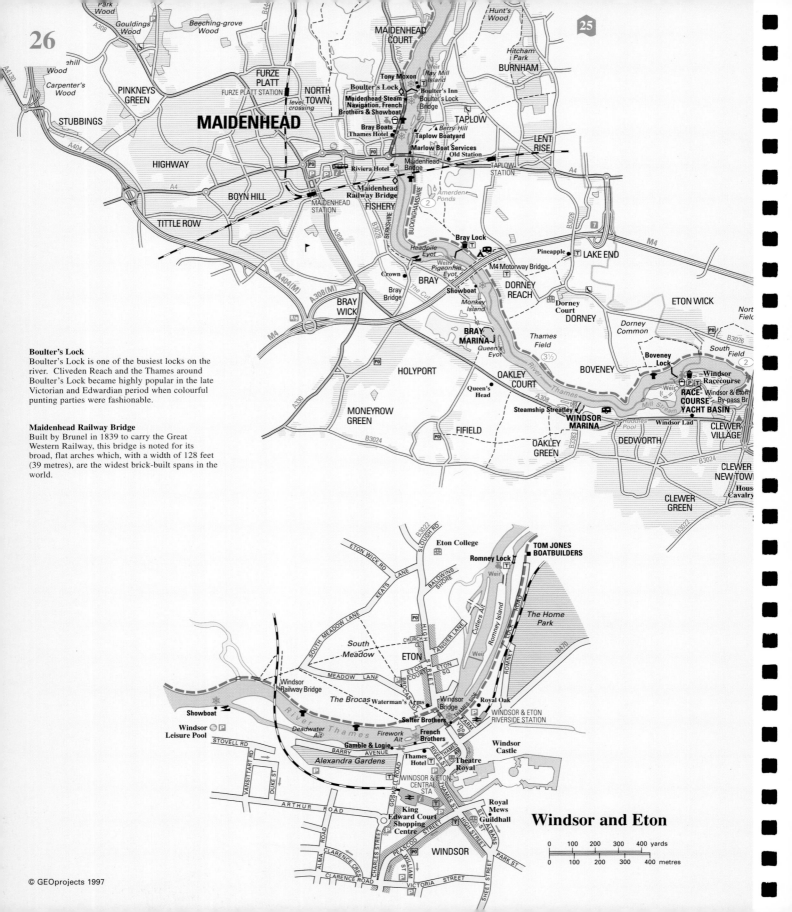

MAIDENHEAD

Boulter's Lock
Boulter's Lock is one of the busiest locks on the river. Cliveden Reach and the Thames around Boulter's Lock became highly popular in the late Victorian and Edwardian period when colourful punting parties were fashionable.

Maidenhead Railway Bridge
Built by Brunel in 1839 to carry the Great Western Railway, this bridge is noted for its broad, flat arches which, with a width of 128 feet (39 metres), are the widest brick-built spans in the world.

Windsor and Eton

0   100   200   300   400 yards

0   100   200   300   400 metres

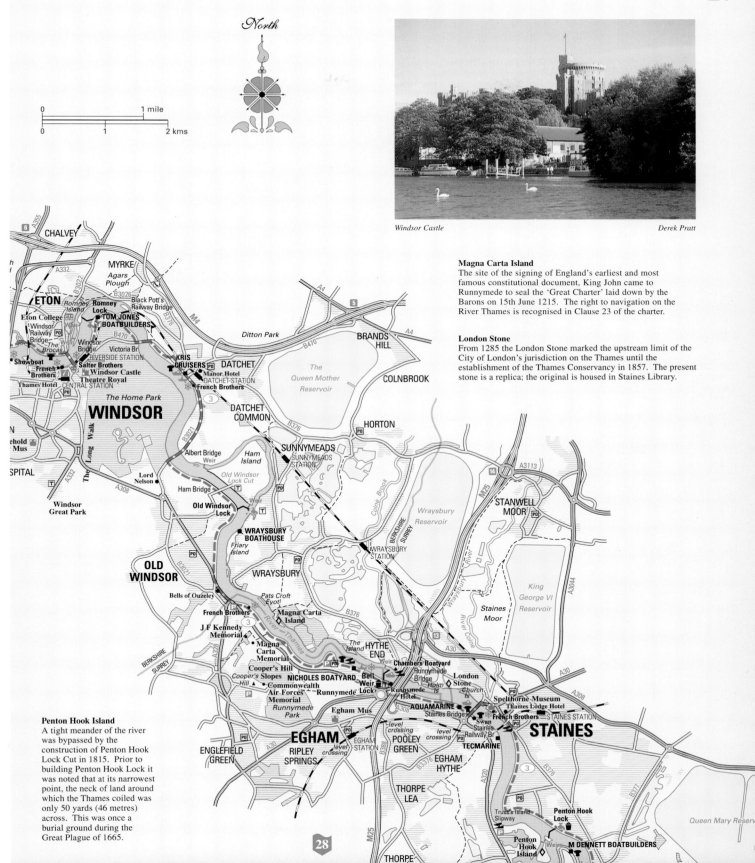

North

Windsor Castle — *Derek Pratt*

Magna Carta Island
The site of the signing of England's earliest and most famous constitutional document, King John came to Runnymede to seal the 'Great Charter' laid down by the Barons on 15th June 1215. The right to navigation on the River Thames is recognised in Clause 23 of the charter.

London Stone
From 1285 the London Stone marked the upstream limit of the City of London's jurisdiction on the Thames until the establishment of the Thames Conservancy in 1857. The present stone is a replica; the original is housed in Staines Library.

Penton Hook Island
A tight meander of the river was bypassed by the construction of Penton Hook Lock Cut in 1815. Prior to building Penton Hook Lock it was noted that at its narrowest point, the neck of land around which the Thames coiled was only 50 yards (46 metres) across. This was once a burial ground during the Great Plague of 1665.

Map labels: CHALVEY, MYRKE, Agars Plough, ETON, Eton College, Windsor Railway Bridge, The Brocas, Showboat, French Brothers, Thames Hotel, Romney Island, Romney Lock, TOM JONES BOATBUILDERS, Black Pott's Railway Bridge, Windsor Bridge, Victoria Br., Salter Brothers, Windsor Castle, Theatre Royal, CENTRAL STATION, RIVERSIDE STATION, The Home Park, WINDSOR, Household Mus, HOSPITAL, The Long Walk, Windsor Great Park, Lord Nelson, Albert Bridge Weir, Ham Island, Ham Bridge, OLD WINDSOR, Old Windsor Lock Cut, Old Windsor Lock, Weir, WRAYSBURY BOATHOUSE, Friary Island, Bells of Ouzeley, French Brothers, J F Kennedy Memorial, Magna Carta Island, Pats Croft Eyot, Magna Carta Memorial, Cooper's Hill, Cooper's Slopes Hill, Commonwealth Air Forces Memorial, Runnymede Park, NICHOLES BOATYARD, Runnymede, Bell Weir Lock, Runnymede Hotel, Holm Is, ENGLEFIELD GREEN, EGHAM, RIPLEY SPRINGS, Egham Mus, EGHAM STATION, POOLEY GREEN, EGHAM HYTHE, THORPE LEA, THORPE, KRIS CRUISERS, DATCHET, Manor Hotel, DATCHET STATION, French Brothers, DATCHET COMMON, Ditton Park, SUNNYMEADS, SUNNYMEADS STATION, BRANDS HILL, COLNBROOK, The Queen Mother Reservoir, HORTON, WRAYSBURY, WRAYSBURY STATION, Berkshire, Surrey, Colne Brook, Wraysbury Reservoir, The Island, HYTHE END, Weir, Chambers Boatyard, Runnymede Bridge, London Stone, Staines Bridge, AQUAMARINE, Swan, Staines Railway Br, TECMARINE, level crossing, STANWELL MOOR, King George VI Reservoir, Staines Moor, River Colne, Wraysbury River, Spelthorne Museum, Thames Lodge Hotel, French Brothers, STAINES STATION, STAINES, Truss's Island Slipway, Penton Hook Lock, Penton Hook Island, M DENNETT BOATBUILDERS, Queen Mary Reservoir, River Thames, Church Is

Scale: 0 — 1 mile, 0 — 1 — 2 kms

Richmond

Desborough Cut

Named in honour of Lord Desborough, the longest serving chairman of the Thames Conservancy (1904-1937), this artificial cut was dug in 1935. Although longer, the original Thames course remains navigable and offers a more attractive and rural route to both boater and towpath walker via Shepperton.

Just upstream of Desborough Cut is Shepperton Lock. The weir stream here is the most southerly point reached by the Thames.

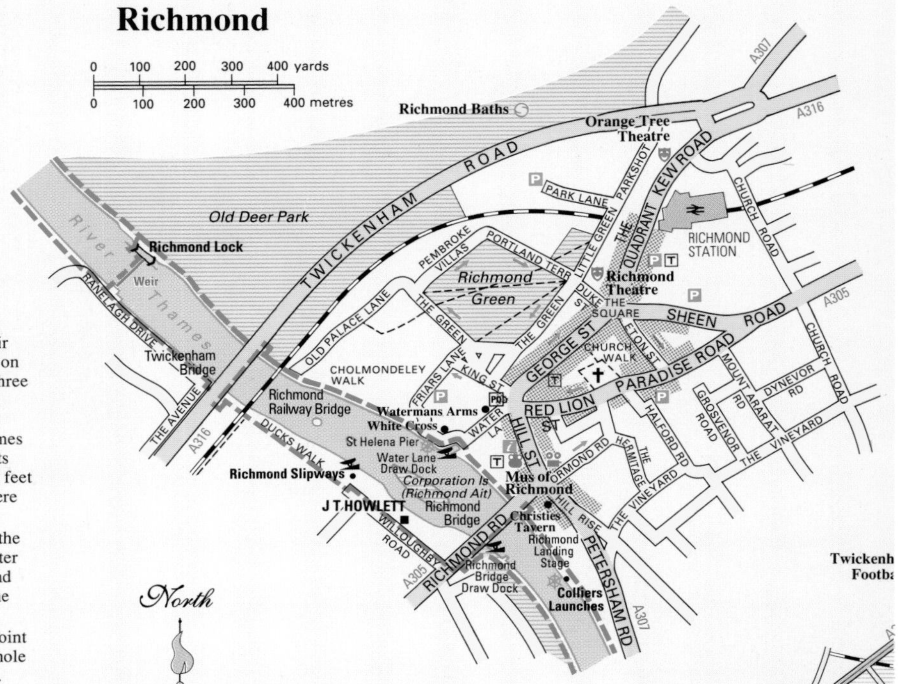

Teddington Locks

Teddington has the longest weir and the largest locking system on the River Thames. There are three locks: Teddington Barge Lock, Teddington Old Lock and Teddington Skiff Lock sometimes known as Coffin Lock due to its size. They have a rise/fall of 8 feet 10 inches (2.68 metres) and were all rebuilt in 1931.

The locks at Teddington mark the transition between the freshwater Thames of the pleasure boat and the commercial waterway of the tidal Thames.

Teddington is also a gauging point of crucial importance to the whole river and especially to London. An average daily discharge of 1,535,000,000 gallons of water pour over Teddington Weir. The monitoring station here is responsible for issuing flood warnings for the Thames and its tributaries.

North

GEO projects
for full details of navigating or walking to Pyrford or Odiham please see GEOprojects map of the BASINGSTOKE CANAL

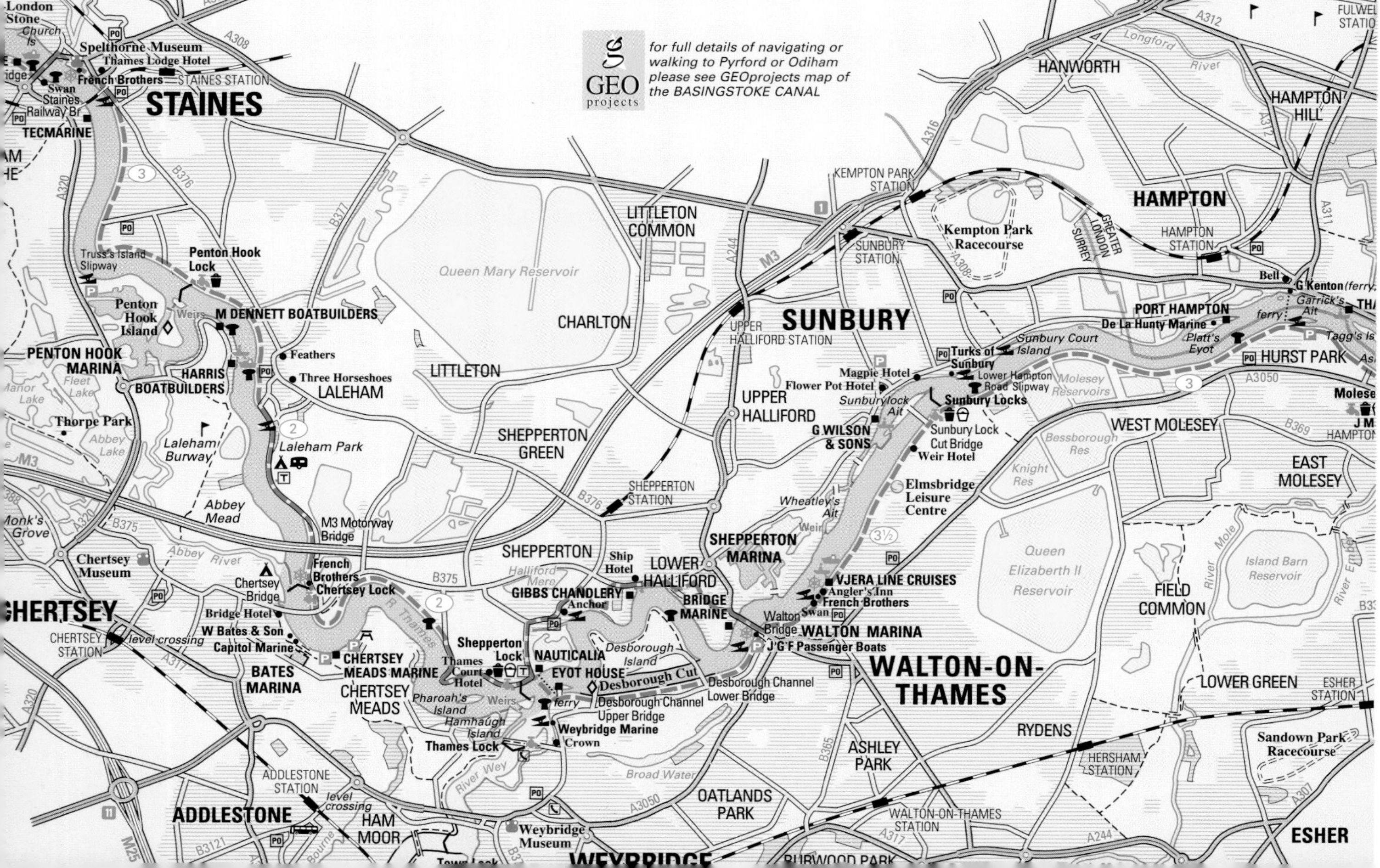

(Map of the River Thames region including Richmond, Staines, Chertsey, Shepperton, Sunbury, Hampton, Walton-on-Thames, Weybridge, Addlestone and surrounding areas. Scale bars show 0–400 yards and 0–400 metres.)

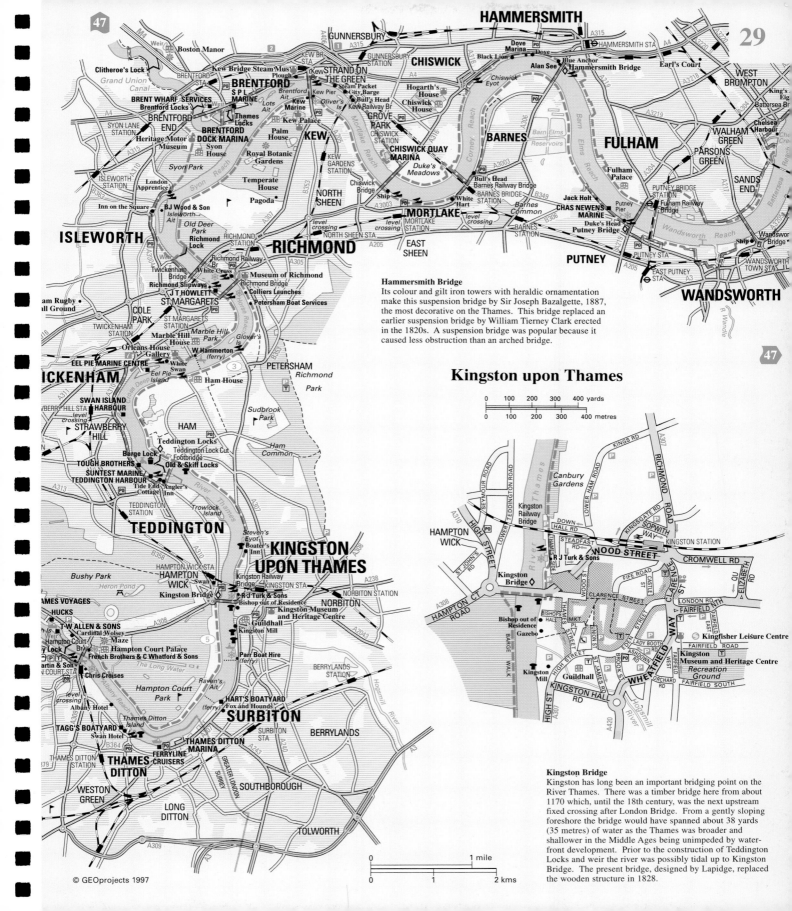

Hammersmith Bridge
Its colour and gilt iron towers with heraldic ornamentation make this suspension bridge by Sir Joseph Bazalgette, 1887, the most decorative on the Thames. This bridge replaced an earlier suspension bridge by William Tierney Clark erected in the 1820s. A suspension bridge was popular because it caused less obstruction than an arched bridge.

Kingston upon Thames

Kingston Bridge
Kingston has long been an important bridging point on the River Thames. There was a timber bridge here from about 1170 which, until the 18th century, was the next upstream fixed crossing after London Bridge. From a gently sloping foreshore the bridge would have spanned about 38 yards (35 metres) of water as the Thames was broader and shallower in the Middle Ages being unimpeded by waterfront development. Prior to the construction of Teddington Locks and weir the river was possibly tidal up to Kingston Bridge. The present bridge, designed by Lapidge, replaced the wooden structure in 1828.

© GEOprojects 1997

Grand Union Canal

OXFORD CANAL

GRAND UNION CANAL

RIVER THAMES

The Thames Ring is completed by the Grand Union Canal from Braunston to London, the main line reaching the Thames at Brentford, a distance of 93½ miles (150 km) with 102 locks. From Bull's Bridge Junction the London Ring follows the Paddington Arm to Little Venice and then the Regent's Canal to join the Thames at Limehouse, 22 miles (35.5 km) and 13 locks away. The 6 miles (9.5 km) and 12 locks of the canal between Bull's Bridge Junction and Brentford is common to both rings.

Climbing up Braunston Locks the Grand Union reaches its first summit level and passes through Braunston Tunnel, 2042 yards (1867 metres) long, before descending the Buckby Locks, parallel to the M1 motorway. Beyond Blisworth Tunnel, 3057 yards (2795 metres) long, the canal passes down the Stoke Bruerne Locks. After Cosgrove Lock the canal enters Fenny Pound ahead of the long ascent by way of 24 locks to its second summit level at Tring. Here the Grand Union Canal carves its way through the chalk of the Chilterns in a 1½ mile (2.5 km) cutting, beginning its fall to the River Thames at Cowroast Lock. South of Hemel Hempstead the course of the canal uses the River Gade between locks 66 and 76, then the River Colne through the water filled gravel workings west of Harefield and, finally, the River Brent which enters the canal just below Hanwell Bottom Lock.

History

Built as the Grand Junction Canal by engineer William Jessop (1745-1814), this 'broad' navigation opened in 1800. It was designed as a direct, efficient route between the Oxford Canal at Braunston and the capital for transporting coal, raw materials and agricultural produce, cutting the distance to London via the Oxford Canal - River Thames route by some 60 miles (97 km).

Railway competition began in 1838 with the opening of the London - Birmingham Line. Measures taken by the Grand Junction Canal Company to improve navigation, speed up traffic and remain competitive included duplicating the Stoke Bruerne Locks in 1835, using steam tugs to haul boats through Braunston and Blisworth Tunnels from 1871 and lowering tolls. Commercial carrying survived into the twentieth century.

The Grand Union Canal came into being on 1st January 1929 when the Regent's Canal Company acquired the Grand Junction Canal which had merged with the neighbouring 'Warwick Canals' and 'Leicestershire Navigations' in an amalgamation of eleven different companies. British Waterways is the navigation authority for the Grand Union Canal.

Look out for

◇ **Braunston Marina** The main entrance to Braunston Marina, now on the Grand Union Canal, is part of the old course of the Oxford Canal abandoned after the straightening programme completed in 1834. The Oxford and Grand Union Canals now meet at Braunston Turn.

◇ **Canal Museum** The Canal Museum at Stoke Bruerne opened in 1963 and is housed in a converted corn mill. Exhibits including a reconstructed butty boat, traditional costumes and ornate rope work trace the 200 year history of the canals.

◇ **Fenny Stratford** A typical canal village setting with a lock, moorings, canalside pub - the Red Lion, and railway bridge, now sandwiched between the urban spread of Bletchley and Milton Keynes.

◇ **Tring Reservoirs** Three reservoirs (Marsworth, Tringford and Startop's End) in peaceful countryside are managed to supply water to the canal as well as a nature reserve with a 2 mile (3 km) nature trail and public hide for observing the varied bird life.

◇ **London Canal Museum** Opened in 1992 the museum relates the importance of London's waterways in the development of the capital, occupying the former warehouse of the famous Swiss-Italian ice cream manufacturer Carlo Gatti.

Canal Societies

The Grand Union Canal Society was formed in 1967 to promote the use, preservation, restoration and a sympathetic development of the canal and to encourage and support all public and private bodies in this task through public meetings, exhibitions, publications and voluntary working parties.

Grand Union Canal Society
PO Box 254
Hemel Hempstead
Herts HP1 2SU
Tel: 01442 872217

Brent River and Canal Society
17 Sutherland Road
Ealing
London W13 0DX
Tel: 0181 998 9785

Leighton Buzzard Canal Society
41 Himley Green
Linslade
Beds
Tel: 01525 374498

Paddington Waterways and
Maida Vale Society
25 Ashworth Road
Maida Vale
London W9 1JW
Tel: 0171 286 5230

The Stop House, British Waterways Office, Braunston   *Derek Pratt*

Marina and Boatyard Facilities

	Long term mooring	Temporary/over-night mooring	Slipway	Water	Refuse disposal	Elsan disposal	Pump out	Electricity points	Bottled gas	Diesel	Boat/engine repairs	Cranage	Hardstanding	Parts and equipment	Boat sales	Chandlery/shop
Braunston Marina Tel: 01788 891373	■	■		■	■	■	■	■	■	■	■	■	■	■	■	■
Braunston Boats Tel: 01788 891079	■						■		■	■						■
Union Canal Carriers Tel: 01788 890784	■				■	■	■			■				■		■
Whilton Marina Tel: 01327 842577	■	■	■					■	■							■
Concoform Marine Tel: 01327 340739	■			■			■		■							
Stowe Hill Marine Tel: 01327 341365	■							■		■						
Waterways Services Tel: 01327 342300	■	■		■	■	■	■									
Grand Junction Boat Co Tel: 01604 858043			■				■	■		■			■			■
Blisworth Tunnel Boats Tel: 01604 858868	■	■		■		■	■	■	■	■			■			■
Baxter Boat-Fitting Services Tel: 01908 542822	■	■		■		■	■	■	■	■			■			■
Cosgrove Marina Tel: 01908 562467	■	■	■	■	■	■	■	■	■	■	■	■	■	■	■	■
Milton Keynes Marina Tel: 01908 672672	■	■		■	■	■	■	■	■	■	■		■			■
Willowbridge Enterprises Tel: 01908 643242	■	■		■	■	■	■	■	■	■			■			■
Wyvern Shipping Company Tel: 01525 372355	■	■		■			■	■	■	■			■			
Grebe Canal Cruises Tel: 01296 661920	■	■	■	■	■	■	■	■	■	■				■		
Cowroast Marina Tel: 01442 823222	■	■	■	■	■	■	■	■	■	■	■	■	■	■	■	■
Bridgewater Boats Tel: 01442 863615				■									■			
Middx and Herts Boat Services Tel: 01442 872985	■	■		■	■	■	■	■	■	■	■	■	■	■	■	■
Bridgewater Basin Tel: 01923 211448	■	■		■	■		■		■		■					
Harefield Marina Tel: 01895 822036	■	■		■	■	■	■	■	■	■	■	■	■	■		■
Denham Yacht Station Tel: 01895 239811	■	■		■	■		■	■		■	■	■	■	■	■	■
Uxbridge Boat Centre Tel: 01895 252019	■	■	■	■	■			■	■	■			■		■	■
High Line Yachting - Cowley Peachey Tel: 01753 651496	■	■		■	■	■	■	■	■	■	■	■	■	■		■
Adelaide Marine Tel: 0181 571 5678		■		■	■	■	■	■	■	■	■	■	■	■		■
Brent Wharf Services Tel: 0181 568 7041	■	■		■				■	■		■	■	■	■		■
SPL Marine Tel: 0181 560 9326	■									■		■	■	■	■	
Brentford Dock Marina Tel: 0181 568 5096	■	■		■	■		■									
Willowtree Marina Tel: 0181 841 6585	■	■					■	■	■	■		■			■	■
High Line Yachting - Northolt Tel: 01753 651496	■	■		■	■	■		■	■	■	■					
Limehouse Marina Tel: 0171 537 2828	■	■		■	■	■	■									

Maximum Recommended Craft Dimensions

	Length	Beam	Headroom	Draught
Braunston to Berkhamsted	72' 0" 21.95 m	7' 0" 2.13 m	7' 6" 2.28 m	3' 6" 1.06 m
Berkhamsted to Brentford	72' 0" 21.95 m	14' 0" 4.26 m	7' 6" 2.28 m	3' 6" 1.06 m
Paddington Arm & Regents Canal	72' 0" 21.95 m	14' 6" 4.42 m	8' 6" 2.59 m	4' 0 1.22 m

Approaching Braunston   *Derek Pratt*

Directory

Navigation authority:
British Waterways is the navigation authority for the Grand Union Canal

Canal Office:
British Waterways
(Braunston to Stowe Hill)
The Stop House
Braunston
Northamptonshire NN11 7JQ
Tel: 01788 890666

Canal Office:
British Waterways
(Stowe Hill to Cowley)
Marsworth Junction
Watery Lane
Marsworth
Tring
Hertfordshire HP23 4LZ

Canal Office:
British Waterways
(Cowley to Brentford and Limehouse)
The Toll Office
Delamere Terrace
London W2 6ND
Tel: 0171 286 6101

Harbour Master's Office:
British Waterways
Limehouse Basin
Narrow Street
London E14 8DN
Tel: 0171 895 9930

South Region Office:
British Waterways
Brindley House
Corner Hall
Lawn Lane
Hemel Hempstead
Hertfordshire HP3 9YT
Tel: 01442 235400

Headquarters:
British Waterways
Willow Grange
Church Road
Watford
Hertfordshire WD1 3QA
Tel: 01923 226422

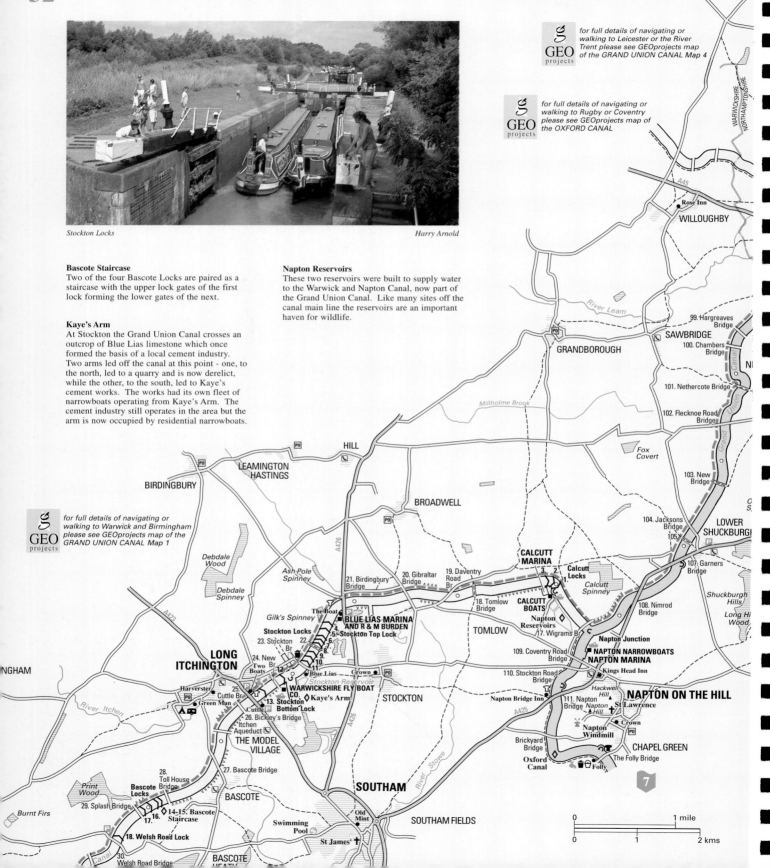

Stockton Locks   Harry Arnold

Bascote Staircase
Two of the four Bascote Locks are paired as a
staircase with the upper lock gates of the first
lock forming the lower gates of the next.

Kaye's Arm
At Stockton the Grand Union Canal crosses an
outcrop of Blue Lias limestone which once
formed the basis of a local cement industry.
Two arms led off the canal at this point - one, to
the north, led to a quarry and is now derelict,
while the other, to the south, led to Kaye's
cement works. The works had its own fleet of
narrowboats operating from Kaye's Arm. The
cement industry still operates in the area but the
arm is now occupied by residential narrowboats.

Napton Reservoirs
These two reservoirs were built to supply water
to the Warwick and Napton Canal, now part of
the Grand Union Canal. Like many sites off the
canal main line the reservoirs are an important
haven for wildlife.

GEO projects
for full details of navigating or
walking to Leicester or the River
Trent please see GEOprojects map
of the GRAND UNION CANAL Map 4

GEO projects
for full details of navigating or
walking to Rugby or Coventry
please see GEOprojects map of
the OXFORD CANAL

GEO projects
for full details of navigating or
walking to Warwick and Birmingham
please see GEOprojects map of the
GRAND UNION CANAL Map 1

WILLOUGHBY
Rose Inn

WARWICKSHIRE
NORTHAMPTONSHIRE

River Leam

99. Hargreaves Bridge
SAWBRIDGE
100. Chambers Bridge
GRANDBOROUGH
101. Nethercote Bridge
102. Flecknoe Road Bridge
Millholme Brook
Fox Covert
103. New Bridge

HILL
LEAMINGTON HASTINGS
BIRDINGBURY
BROADWELL
104. Jacksons Bridge
105.
LOWER SHUCKBURGH

107. Garners Bridge
Debdale Wood
Debdale Spinney
Ash Pole Spinney
21. Birdingbury Bridge
20. Gibraltar Bridge
19. Daventry Road Br.
CALCUTT MARINA
3. 2.
Calcutt Locks
1.
Calcutt Spinney
108. Nimrod Bridge
Shuckburgh Hills
Long Hi Wood

Gilk's Spinney
The Boat
BLUE LIAS MARINA
AND R & M BURDEN
Stockton Top Lock
18. Tomlow Bridge
CALCUTT BOATS
Napton Reservoirs
TOMLOW
17. Wigrams Br.

Stockton Locks
23. Stockton Br.
22.
5.
6.
7.
8.
9.
LONG ITCHINGTON
24. New Two Bridges
12.
11.
10.
Blue Lias
Crown
109. Coventry Road Bridge
NAPTON NARROWBOATS
NAPTON MARINA
Napton Junction

Harvester
25.
Cuttle Br.
Green Man
13. Stockton Bottom Lock
Cuttle
WARWICKSHIRE FLY BOAT CO.
Kaye's Arm
Stockton Reservoir
STOCKTON
110. Stockton Road Bridge
Kings Head Inn
Napton Bridge Inn
111. Napton Bridge
Hackwell Hill
Napton Hill
St Lawrence
NAPTON ON THE HILL

River Itchen
26. Bickley's Bridge
Itchen Aqueduct
THE MODEL VILLAGE
27. Bascote Bridge
A426
River Stowe
Brickyard Bridge
Napton Windmill
Crown
CHAPEL GREEN
The Folly Bridge

Print Wood
28. Toll House Bridge
Bascote Locks
29. Splash Bridge
17. 16.
14-15. Bascote Staircase
18. Welsh Road Lock
BASCOTE
Oxford Canal
Folly
7

SOUTHAM
Old Mint
St James'
SOUTHAM FIELDS

Burnt Firs
30. Welsh Road Bridge
BASCOTE HEATH
Swimming Pool

0   1 mile
0   1   2 kms

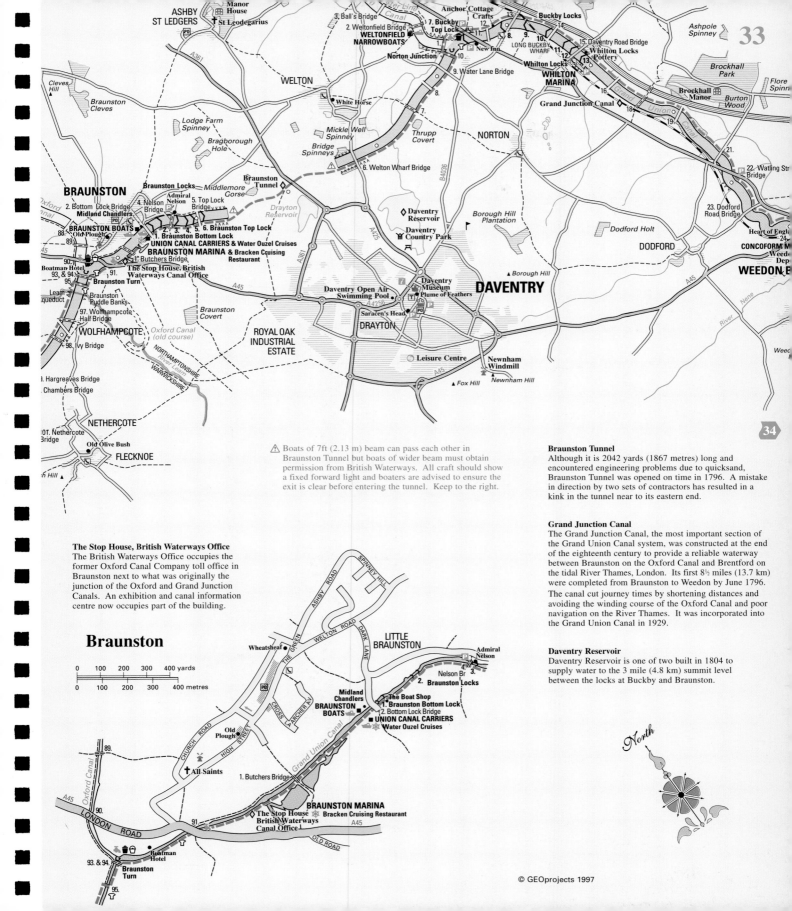

⚠ Boats of 7ft (2.13 m) beam can pass each other in Braunston Tunnel but boats of wider beam must obtain permission from British Waterways. All craft should show a fixed forward light and boaters are advised to ensure the exit is clear before entering the tunnel. Keep to the right.

Braunston Tunnel
Although it is 2042 yards (1867 metres) long and encountered engineering problems due to quicksand, Braunston Tunnel was opened on time in 1796. A mistake in direction by two sets of contractors has resulted in a kink in the tunnel near to its eastern end.

Grand Junction Canal
The Grand Junction Canal, the most important section of the Grand Union Canal system, was constructed at the end of the eighteenth century to provide a reliable waterway between Braunston on the Oxford Canal and Brentford on the tidal River Thames, London. Its first 8½ miles (13.7 km) were completed from Braunston to Weedon by June 1796.

The canal cut journey times by shortening distances and avoiding the winding course of the Oxford Canal and poor navigation on the River Thames. It was incorporated into the Grand Union Canal in 1929.

Daventry Reservoir
Daventry Reservoir is one of two built in 1804 to supply water to the 3 mile (4.8 km) summit level between the locks at Buckby and Braunston.

The Stop House, British Waterways Office
The British Waterways Office occupies the former Oxford Canal Company toll office in Braunston next to what was originally the junction of the Oxford and Grand Junction Canals. An exhibition and canal information centre now occupies part of the building.

Braunston

0   100   200   300   400 yards
0   100   200   300   400 metres

© GEOprojects 1997

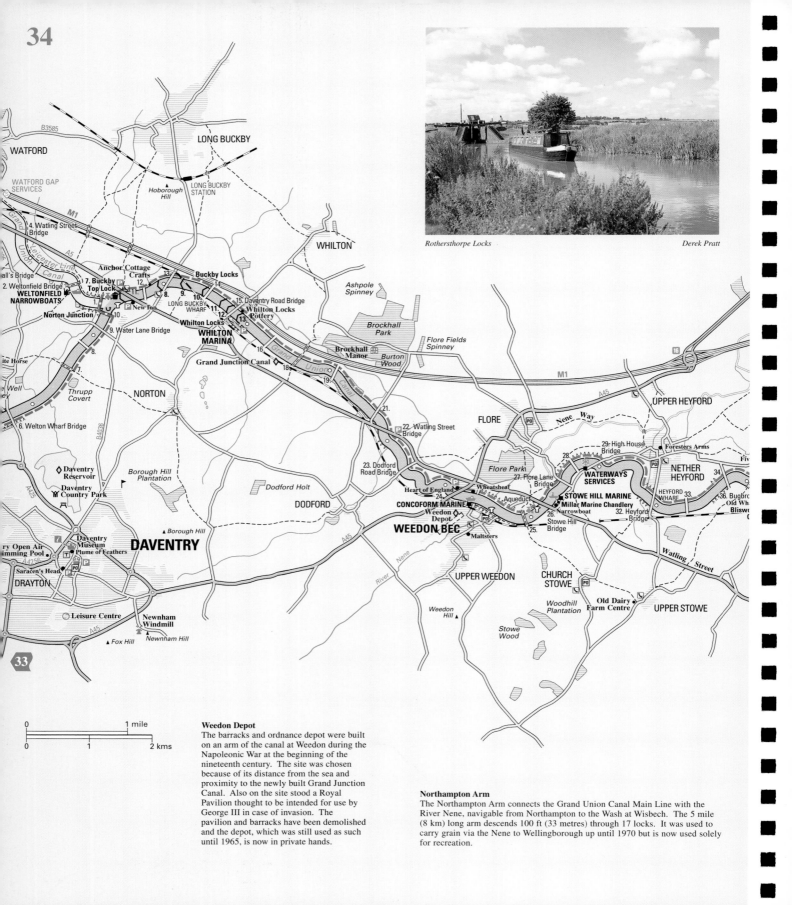

WATFORD

LONG BUCKBY

WATFORD GAP
SERVICES

Hoborough
Hill

LONG BUCKBY
STATION

WHILTON

B3585

M1

A5

4. Watling Street
Bridge

Grand Union Canal

Leicester Line

Anchor Cottage
Crafts

7. Buckby
Top Lock

Buckby Locks

2. Weltonfield Bridge
WELTONFIELD
NARROWBOATS

New Inn

LONG BUCKBY
WHARF

15. Daventry Road Bridge
Whilton Locks
Pottery

Norton Junction

9. Water Lane Bridge

Whilton Locks

WHILTON
MARINA

6. Welton Wharf Bridge

Thrupp
Covert

NORTON

Grand Junction Canal

Grand Union Canal

Ashpole
Spinney

Brockhall
Park

Brockhall
Manor

Burton
Wood

Flore Fields
Spinney

M1

16

UPPER HEYFORD

A45

FLORE

Nene Way

29. High House
Bridge

Foresters Arms

28

NETHER
HEYFORD

34

Daventry
Reservoir

Daventry
Country Park

Borough Hill
Plantation

Dodford Holt

Flore Park

Flore Lane
Bridge

22. Watling Street
Bridge

23. Dodford
Road Bridge

WATERWAYS
SERVICES

STOWE HILL MARINE

Millar Marine Chandlery

Narrowboat

32. Heyford
Bridge

HEYFORD
WHARF

33

36. Bugbro
Old Wh
Bliswo

Daventry
Museum

Plume of Feathers

DAVENTRY

Borough Hill

DODFORD

Heart of England

Wheatsheaf

Aqueduct

CONCOFORM MARINE

Weedon
Depot

WEEDON BEC

26

25

Stowe Hill
Bridge

Five

ry Open Air
mming Pool

Saracen's Head

DRAYTON

A425

A4256

Leisure Centre

Newnham
Windmill

Fox Hill

Newnham Hill

A45

River Nene

UPPER WEEDON

Maltsters

Weedon
Hill

CHURCH
STOWE

Woodhill
Plantation

Stowe
Wood

Old Dairy

Old Dairy
Farm Centre

UPPER STOWE

Watling Street

Rothersthorpe Locks   *Derek Pratt*

0   1 mile
0   1   2 kms

Weedon Depot
The barracks and ordnance depot were built on an arm of the canal at Weedon during the Napoleonic War at the beginning of the nineteenth century. The site was chosen because of its distance from the sea and proximity to the newly built Grand Junction Canal. Also on the site stood a Royal Pavilion thought to be intended for use by George III in case of invasion. The pavilion and barracks have been demolished and the depot, which was still used as such until 1965, is now in private hands.

Northampton Arm
The Northampton Arm connects the Grand Union Canal Main Line with the River Nene, navigable from Northampton to the Wash at Wisbech. The 5 mile (8 km) long arm descends 100 ft (33 metres) through 17 locks. It was used to carry grain via the Nene to Wellingborough up until 1970 but is now used solely for recreation.

33

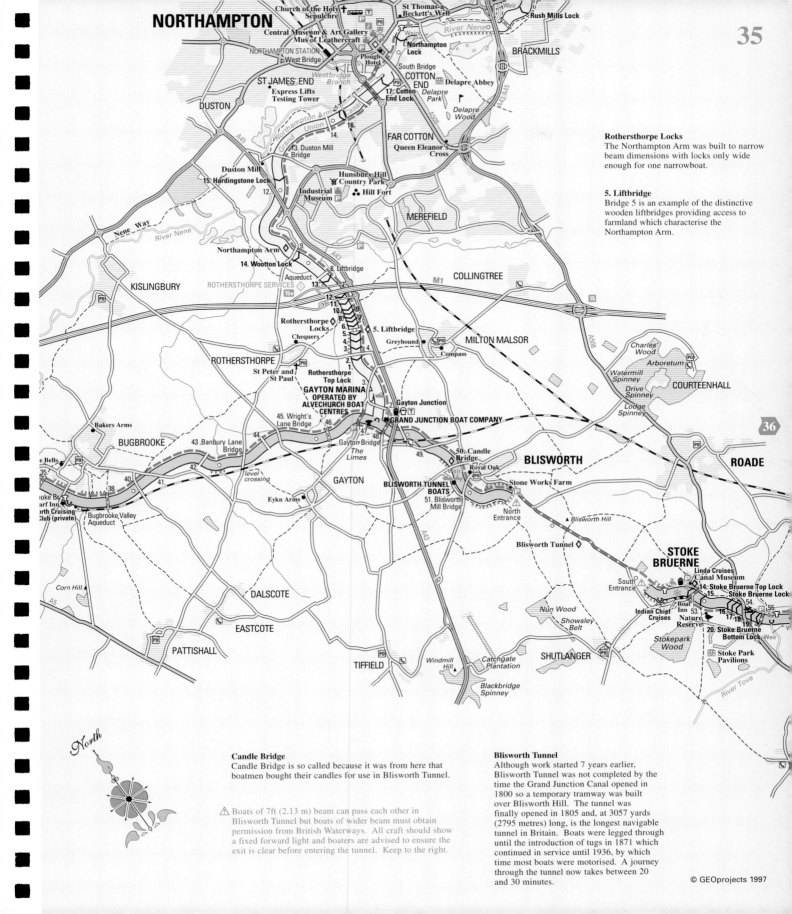

NORTHAMPTON

Church of the Holy Sepulchre
St Thomas-a-Beckett's Well
River Nene
Rush Mills Lock
Weir

Central Museum & Art Gallery
Mus of Leathercraft

NORTHAMPTON STATION
West Bridge
Plough Hotel
Weirs
Northampton Lock
BRACKMILLS

ST JAMES' END
Westbridge Branch
South Bridge
COTTON END
Delapre Abbey

DUSTON
Express Lifts Testing Tower
17. Cotton End Lock
Delapre Park
Delapre Wood

16.
FAR COTTON
Queen Eleanor's Cross
14.
13. Duston Mill Bridge
12.
Duston Mill
15. Hardingstone Lock
Hunsbury Hill Country Park
MEREFIELD
Hill Fort
Industrial Museum

Nene Way
River Nene
Northampton Arm
14. Wootton Lock
8. Liftbridge
COLLINGTREE
M1

KISLINGBURY
Aqueduct
ROTHERSTHORPE SERVICES
13.
15a
12.
11.
10.
9.
8.
7.
6.
5. Liftbridge
Greyhound
MILTON MALSOR
Compass
15

Rothersthorpe Locks
Chequers
5.
4.
3.
Charles' Wood
Arboretum
Watermill Spinney
Drive Spinney
Lodge Spinney
COURTEENHALL

ROTHERSTHORPE
St Peter and St Paul
Rothersthorpe Top Lock
2.
1.
4.
3.
GAYTON MARINA
OPERATED BY ALVECHURCH BOAT CENTRES
Bakers Arms
2.
Gayton Junction
45. Wright's Lane Bridge
46.
GRAND JUNCTION BOAT COMPANY
36

BUGBROOKE
43. Banbury Lane Bridge
44.
47.
48.
Gayton Bridge
The Limes
49.
50. Candle Bridge
BLISWORTH
ROADE

42.
level crossing
GAYTON
51. Blisworth Mill Bridge
Royal Oak
BLISWORTH TUNNEL BOATS
Weir
North Entrance
Stone Works Farm

35.
40.
41.
Eykn Arms
Blisworth Hill
Blisworth Tunnel

Bugbrooke Valley Aqueduct
38.
North Cruising Club (private)
roke Bo...
arf Inn

Corn Hill
DALSCOTE
EASTCOTE
Nun Wood
Showsley Belt
STOKE BRUERNE
Linda Cruises
Canal Museum
14. Stoke Bruerne Top Lock
15. Stoke Bruerne Lock
16.
54.
South Entrance
Boat Inn
53.
Indian Chief Cruises
Nature Reserve
17. 18.
19.
55.
20. Stoke Bruerne Bottom Lock
Weir
Stokepark Wood
Stoke Park Pavilions

PATTISHALL
TIFFIELD
Windmill Hill
Catchgate Plantation
SHUTLANGER
Blackbridge Spinney
River Tove

North

Rothersthorpe Locks
The Northampton Arm was built to narrow beam dimensions with locks only wide enough for one narrowboat.

5. Liftbridge
Bridge 5 is an example of the distinctive wooden liftbridges providing access to farmland which characterise the Northampton Arm.

Candle Bridge
Candle Bridge is so called because it was from here that boatmen bought their candles for use in Blisworth Tunnel.

⚠ Boats of 7ft (2.13 m) beam can pass each other in Blisworth Tunnel but boats of wider beam must obtain permission from British Waterways. All craft should show a fixed forward light and boaters are advised to ensure the exit is clear before entering the tunnel. Keep to the right.

Blisworth Tunnel
Although work started 7 years earlier, Blisworth Tunnel was not completed by the time the Grand Junction Canal opened in 1800 so a temporary tramway was built over Blisworth Hill. The tunnel was finally opened in 1805 and, at 3057 yards (2795 metres) long, is the longest navigable tunnel in Britain. Boats were legged through until the introduction of tugs in 1871 which continued in service until 1936, by which time most boats were motorised. A journey through the tunnel now takes between 20 and 30 minutes.

© GEOprojects 1997

Canal Museum

The Canal Museum in Stoke Bruerne is housed in a converted corn mill and was opened in 1963 to display the collections of former lock keeper Jack James and engineer Charles Hadlow. Exhibits tracing the 200 year history of canals include a reconstructed butty boat 'Sunny Valley', a boat weighing machine, many examples of roses and castles painting, ornate rope work and traditional costumes.

The museum is open daily 10.00 to 18.00 in summer and Tuesday to Sunday, 10.00 to 16.00 in winter.

Old Stratford and Buckingham Arms

The Old Stratford and Buckingham Arms were opened in 1801 to transport coal, stone, hay, straw and other agricultural produce from Watling Street and Buckingham. Together the arms were 10 miles (16.1 km) long and had 2 locks. Trade began to decline with the opening of the nearby railway and the arms suffered problems with silting near to Buckingham. By 1900 all trade as far as Buckingham had ceased and the canal began to lose water through leakage. To avoid loss of water from the Main Line a temporary dam was set up which remained in place until the Old Stratford and Buckingham Arms were officially abandoned in 1964.

All that remains navigable today is a short arm used for moorings but the towpath exists as a public footpath for most of its length. The Buckingham Canal Society was founded in 1992 to promote interest in the canal with the eventual aim of restoring navigation.

Morris Dancers, Canal Museum, Stoke Bruerne *Derek Pratt*

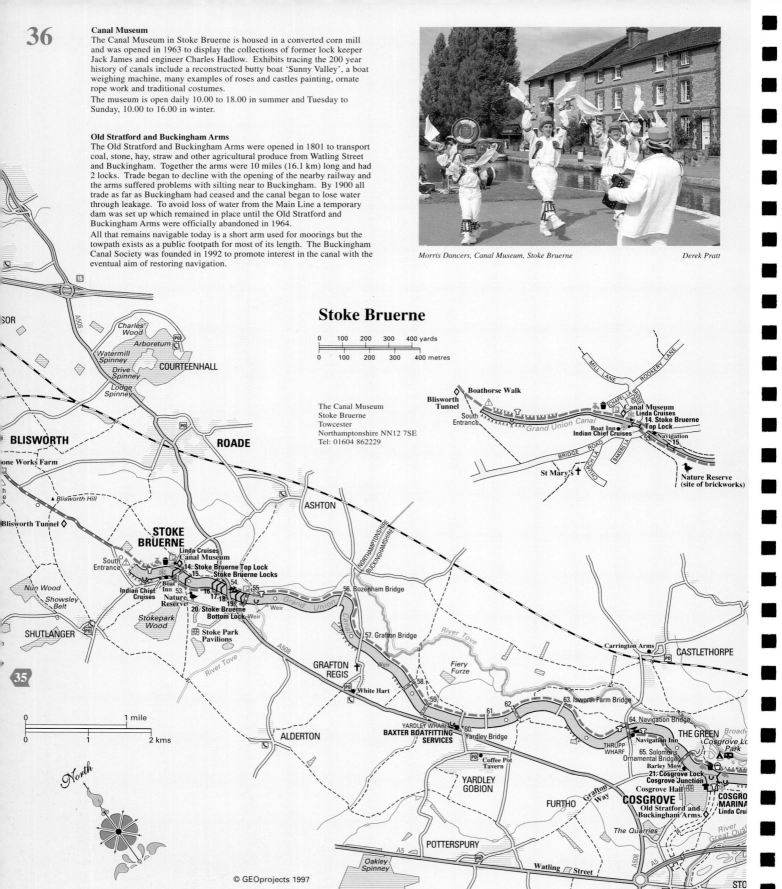

The Canal Museum
Stoke Bruerne
Towcester
Northamptonshire NN12 7SE
Tel: 01604 862229

© GEOprojects 1997

Iron Trunk Aqueduct

When the Grand Junction Canal was first opened a flight of nine temporary locks carried the canal across the Ouse Valley while work was finished on the first aqueduct, built of brick. It was completed in 1805 but part of the embankment collapsed only 5 months later leading to arguments about poor workmanship. In 1808 the entire aqueduct collapsed and the temporary locks had to be brought back into use. It was decided to use a new technique to construct a cast iron replacement which was opened in 1811 and is now a scheduled Ancient Monument.

Linford Wharf

Linford Wharf marks the site where the now abandoned Newport Pagnell Branch once joined the Grand Union Canal Main Line. Completed in 1817, the initial success of this 1¼ mile (2 km) branch was based on the carrying of coal but in the end it could not compete with the railway and was closed in 1864. The Newport Pagnell Railway Company built a line over the abandoned course of the Canal in 1867 but this also proved to be a failure and the route now forms part of the Grand Junction Canal Trail.

Brick Kilns

The Brick Kilns at Great Linford were built in the late 1800s and formed part of an extensive brickmaking industry in the Milton Keynes area which began in the late fifteenth century. The industry provided bricks and floor tiles for many local buildings including Great Linford Manor House. Clay was extracted locally and the canal was used to transport coal and the finished bricks until 1911 when this particular type of kiln was no longer economical.

Great Linford

Pennyland Marina

During the development of Milton Keynes the planners attempted to integrate the canal with the new housing at Pennyland Marina providing residents with private moorings.

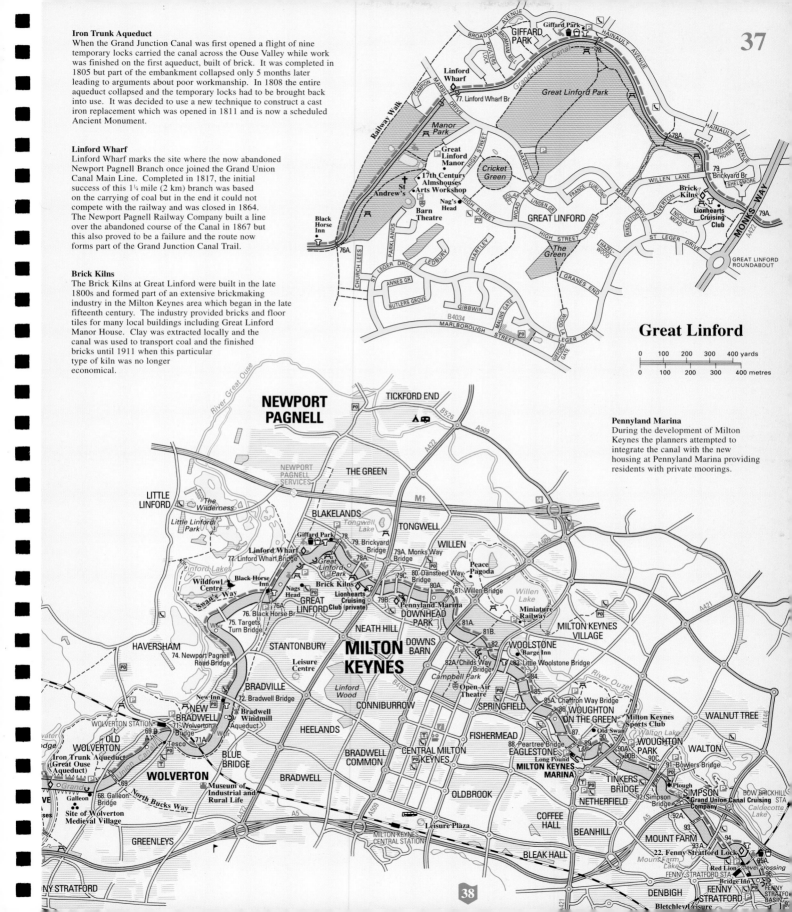

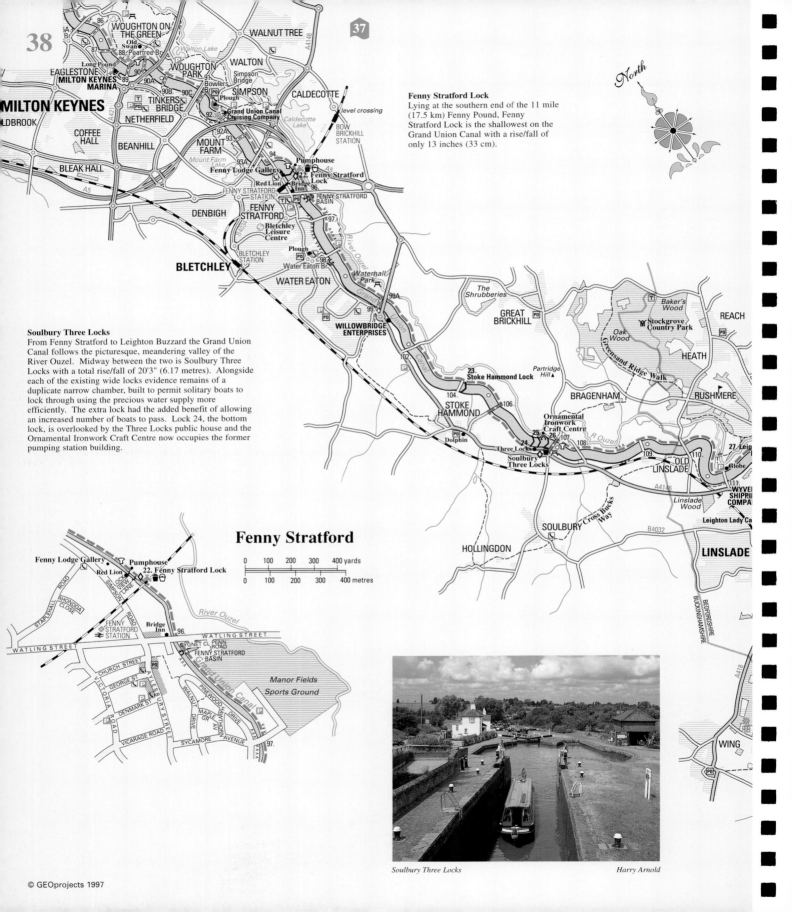

37

North

Fenny Stratford Lock

Lying at the southern end of the 11 mile (17.5 km) Fenny Pound, Fenny Stratford Lock is the shallowest on the Grand Union Canal with a rise/fall of only 13 inches (33 cm).

Soulbury Three Locks

From Fenny Stratford to Leighton Buzzard the Grand Union Canal follows the picturesque, meandering valley of the River Ouzel. Midway between the two is Soulbury Three Locks with a total rise/fall of 20'3" (6.17 metres). Alongside each of the existing wide locks evidence remains of a duplicate narrow chamber, built to permit solitary boats to lock through using the precious water supply more efficiently. The extra lock had the added benefit of allowing an increased number of boats to pass. Lock 24, the bottom lock, is overlooked by the Three Locks public house and the Ornamental Ironwork Craft Centre now occupies the former pumping station building.

Fenny Stratford

| 0 | 100 | 200 | 300 | 400 yards |
| 0 | 100 | 200 | 300 | 400 metres |

Soulbury Three Locks   *Harry Arnold*

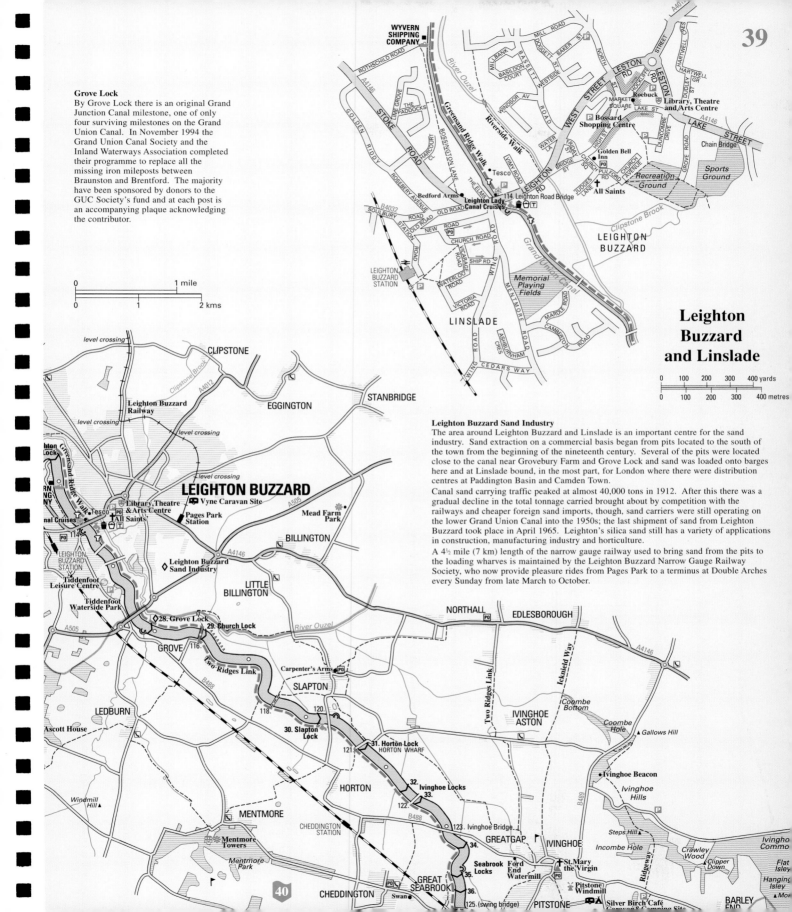

Grove Lock

By Grove Lock there is an original Grand Junction Canal milestone, one of only four surviving milestones on the Grand Union Canal. In November 1994 the Grand Union Canal Society and the Inland Waterways Association completed their programme to replace all the missing iron mileposts between Braunston and Brentford. The majority have been sponsored by donors to the GUC Society's fund and at each post is an accompanying plaque acknowledging the contributor.

Leighton Buzzard and Linslade

Leighton Buzzard Sand Industry

The area around Leighton Buzzard and Linslade is an important centre for the sand industry. Sand extraction on a commercial basis began from pits located to the south of the town from the beginning of the nineteenth century. Several of the pits were located close to the canal near Grovebury Farm and Grove Lock and sand was loaded onto barges here and at Linslade bound, in the most part, for London where there were distribution centres at Paddington Basin and Camden Town.

Canal sand carrying traffic peaked at almost 40,000 tons in 1912. After this there was a gradual decline in the total tonnage carried brought about by competition with the railways and cheaper foreign sand imports, though, sand carriers were still operating on the lower Grand Union Canal into the 1950s; the last shipment of sand from Leighton Buzzard took place in April 1965. Leighton's silica sand still has a variety of applications in construction, manufacturing industry and horticulture.

A 4½ mile (7 km) length of the narrow gauge railway used to bring sand from the pits to the loading wharves is maintained by the Leighton Buzzard Narrow Gauge Railway Society, who now provide pleasure rides from Pages Park to a terminus at Double Arches every Sunday from late March to October.

LEIGHTON BUZZARD

Tring Reservoirs

Collectively Marsworth, Tringford and Startop's End Reservoirs, built in 1806, 1816 and 1817 respectively, are known as the Tring Reservoirs. In addition to providing an essential source of water, Tring Reservoirs are managed as a nature reserve. Tringford Reservoir has a public hide from where resident and migrant ducks and waders can be observed. There is also a 2 mile (3 km) nature trail providing the opportunity to see some of the plants, birds, butterflies and dragonflies that live in a variety of habitats afforded by the reservoirs.

Tring Cutting

Tring Cutting, part of the Tring Summit Pound between Marsworth Top Lock, number 45, and Cowroast Lock, number 46, takes the canal across the chalk ridge of the Chilterns forming the highest point of the Main Line some 395 feet (120 metres) above the Thames at Limehouse. The cutting itself stretches for 1½ miles (2.5 km) and at its maximum is 30 feet (9 metres) deep.

Tringford Pumping Station

Located at the head of navigation on the Wendover Arm, this pumping station was built to raise water from Tringford and Wilstone Reservoirs, situated below the height of the summit level, to the Main Line at Bulbourne Junction via the Wendover Arm.

The original pumps at Tringford were operated by large beam engines, replaced earlier this century by diesel ones which in turn have been superseded by electrically driven pumps. An average of 4 million gallons of water is pumped daily up to the Tring Summit Pound.

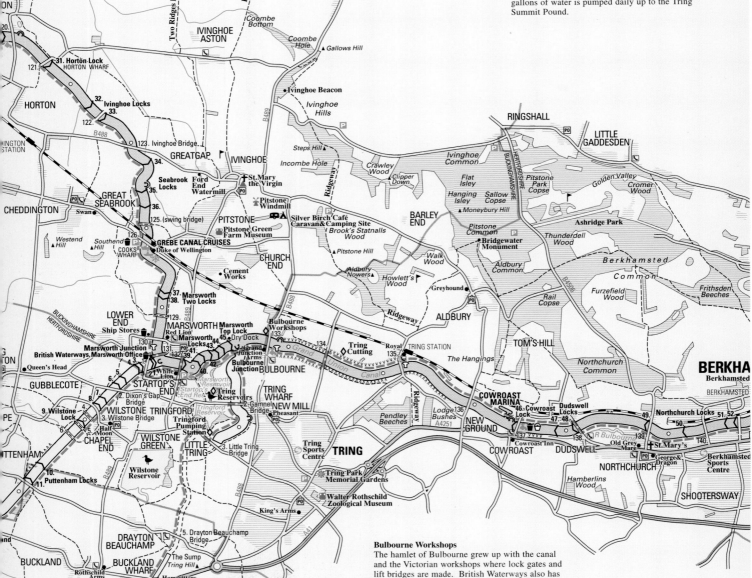

Bulbourne Workshops

The hamlet of Bulbourne grew up with the canal and the Victorian workshops where lock gates and lift bridges are made. British Waterways also has a maintenance base here. There is an annual open weekend in July when the public can see the processes and various stages in the production of traditional wooden lock gates.

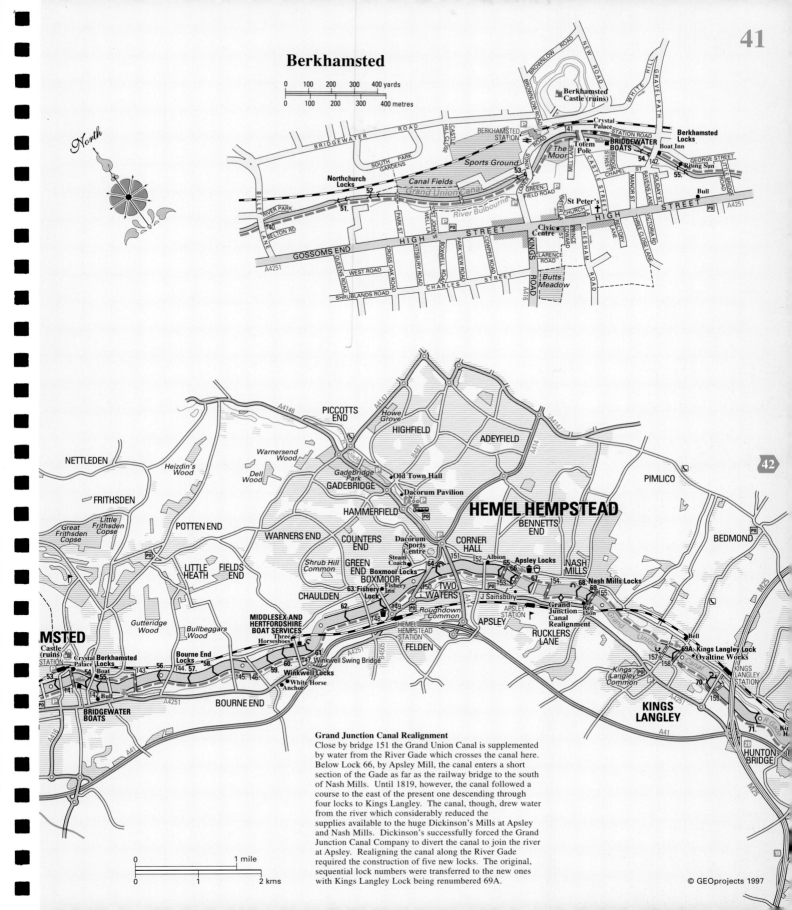

Berkhamsted

Scale bars:
0 100 200 300 400 yards
0 100 200 300 400 metres

Grand Junction Canal Realignment

Close by bridge 151 the Grand Union Canal is supplemented by water from the River Gade which crosses the canal here. Below Lock 66, by Apsley Mill, the canal enters a short section of the Gade as far as the railway bridge to the south of Nash Mills. Until 1819, however, the canal followed a course to the east of the present one descending through four locks to Kings Langley. The canal, though, drew water from the river which considerably reduced the supplies available to the huge Dickinson's Mills at Apsley and Nash Mills. Dickinson's successfully forced the Grand Junction Canal Company to divert the canal to join the river at Apsley. Realigning the canal along the River Gade required the construction of five new locks. The original, sequential lock numbers were transferred to the new ones with Kings Langley Lock being renumbered 69A.

© GEOprojects 1997

Grove Bridge

Commonly known as Ornamental Bridge this balustraded, white painted, stone bridge is one of the most striking bridges on the Grand Union Canal. Grove Bridge is the most decorative of a series of ornamental features along this section of canal, built by the Grand Junction Canal Company for permission for the line of the canal to pass through the estates of the Earl of Clarendon (Grove Park) and the Earl of Essex (Cassiobury Park).

Originally a tunnel of approximately half a mile in length had been planned. This vast expense was avoided and the route of the canal through these landscaped parks was secured with payments of £5,000 to Lord Clarendon and £15,000 to Lord Essex with the condition that this stretch of canal be made as ornamental as possible.

Grove Bridge, number 164.

Derek Pratt

River Chess

Approaching Batchworth Lock, number 81, from the south, the canal towpath is carried over the entrance to the River Chess by a foot-bridge, just beyond which is the lock marking the start of this short, navigable backwater which served Rickmansworth town wharves, a gas works and gravel pits. There is an interesting lift bridge after this lock.

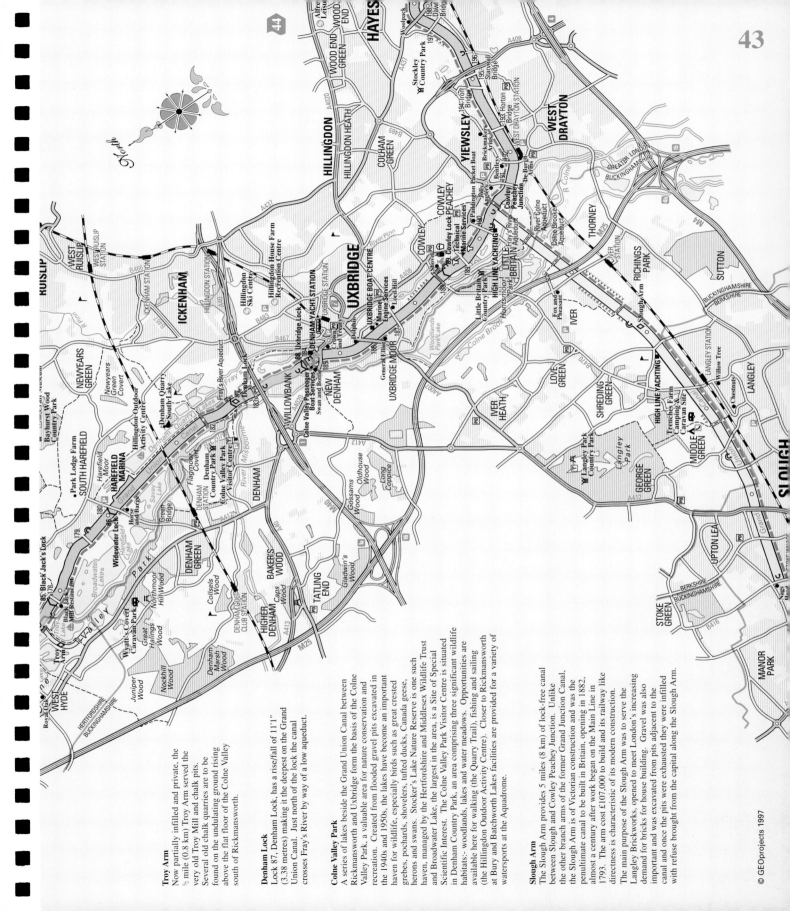

Troy Arm

Now partially infilled and private, the ½ mile (0.8 km) Troy Arm served the very old Troy Mill and chalk pits. Several old chalk quarries are to be found on the undulating ground rising above the flat floor of the Colne Valley south of Rickmansworth.

Denham Lock

Lock 87, Denham Lock, has a rise/fall of 11'1" (3.38 metres) making it the deepest on the Grand Union Canal. Just north of the lock the canal crosses Fray's River by way of a low aqueduct.

Colne Valley Park

A series of lakes beside the Grand Union Canal between Rickmansworth and Uxbridge form the basis of the Colne Valley Park, a valuable area for nature conservation and recreation. Created from flooded gravel pits excavated in the 1940s and 1950s, the lakes have become an important haven for wildlife, especially birds such as great crested grebes, pochards, shovelers, tufted ducks, Canada geese, herons and swans. Stocker's Lake Nature Reserve is one such haven, managed by the Hertfordshire and Middlesex Wildlife Trust and Broadwater Lake, the largest in the area, is a Site of Special Scientific Interest. The Colne Valley Park Visitor Centre is situated in Denham Country Park, an area comprising three significant wildlife habitats:- woodlands, lakes and water meadows. Opportunities are available here for walking (the Quarry Trail), fishing and sailing (the Hillingdon Outdoor Activity Centre). Closer to Rickmansworth at Bury and Batchworth Lakes facilities are provided for a variety of watersports at the Aquadrome.

Slough Arm

The Slough Arm provides 5 miles (8 km) of lock-free canal between Slough and Cowley Peachey Junction. Unlike the other branch arms of the former Grand Junction Canal, the Slough Arm is of Victorian construction and was the penultimate canal to be built in Britain, opening in 1882, almost a century after work began on the Main Line in 1793. The arm cost £107,000 to build and its railway like directness is characteristic of its modern construction. The main purpose of the Slough Arm was to serve the Langley Brickworks, opened to meet London's increasing demand for bricks for house building. Gravel was also important and was excavated from pits adjacent to the canal and once the pits were exhausted they were infilled with refuse brought from the capital along the Slough Arm.

Paddington Arm

The Grand Junction Canal Company realised that it would be desirable to have a canal route into Central London to supplement the way via Brentford, along the River Thames. The Bill authorising the Paddington Arm received Royal Assent in 1795 and construction of the 13½ mile (21.5 km) lock-free canal took six years to complete and opened in July 1801.

The Paddington Arm joins the Grand Union Canal Main Line at Bull's Bridge Junction and passes through the mainly built-up industrial and residential areas of West London to terminate at Paddington Basin, half a mile beyond Browning's Pool. Bull's Bridge Junction developed as a coal trans-shipment point where coal brought down the Grand Junction Canal by narrowboat was loaded onto larger barges bound for Brentford and London. The Grand Union Canal Company made Bull's Bridge a repair yard for their fleet of narrowboats and during the Second World War women recruited to work on the canals were trained here.

The Paddington Arm was noted for its brick carrying traffic and the canal played a key role in transporting building materials to the capital. The Grand Junction Canal Company advertised the prevalence of good brick making earth and the West Drayton, Yiewsley and Hayes canal frontages were dominated by brick fields with their kilns and lines of drying bricks.

Lyon's Dock

Lyon's Dock is situated among the factory buildings of the Lyon's works between bridges 15 and 16 and was the last of the docks built on the Paddington Arm, opening in 1926. The dock is private and the entrance is barred at water level.

Windmill Bridge

Bridge 205, Windmill Bridge, is also known as Three Bridges because three modes of transport meet at this point. The main A4127 road crosses the canal here which in turn bridges a railway freight line. Designed in 1859 by Isambard Kingdom Brunel, it is a unique feature of London's canal heritage and is now a scheduled Ancient Monument.

Port-a-Bella Dock

Port-a-Bella Dock, Kensal Town, was constructed for the Royal Borough of Kensington in 1894 as a loading point for the Borough's refuse which was carried by barge along the Paddington Arm to West Drayton.

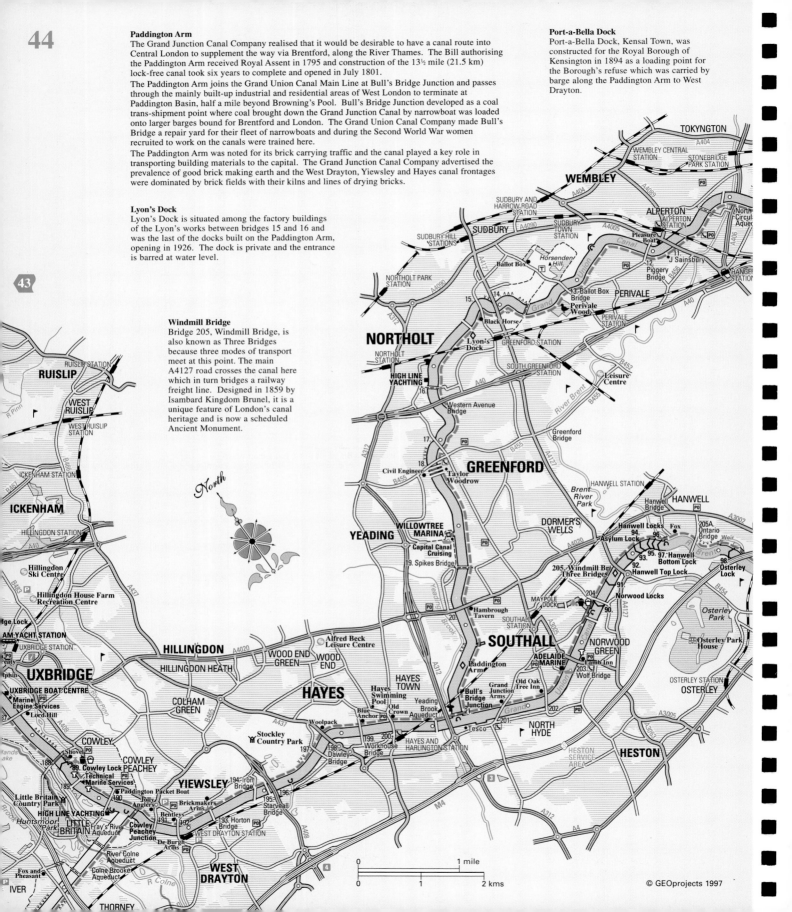

© GEOprojects 1997

Paddington Basin

Following the completion of the Paddington Arm, wharves were laid out and warehouses built at the canal's terminus and Paddington Basin rapidly developed into a thriving inland port with a catchment area for distribution covering all parts of London. In the early part of the 19th century the canal's trade was considerable and an enormous variety of commodities arrived here from all over the country. Stone was carried from Yorkshire and Derbyshire, nails from Derby, glass from Stourbridge, salt from Cheshire, pottery from Staffordshire and light goods were brought from Manchester and Birmingham. This supplemented the principal cargoes of coal, bricks, timber, lime, iron and agricultural produce - Paddington Basin had a flourishing cattle market. Outwards from London were carried manufactured and imported goods and groceries bound for the Midlands. After a gradual decline following the rise of the railways Paddington Basin fell into disuse by the 1920s. The basin has now been renovated to provide moorings.

⚠ Maida Hill Tunnel has no towpath.

Little Venice

Little Venice is centred on the junction of the Paddington Arm, the Regent's Canal and the short arm to Paddington Basin. The triangular area of water thus formed and the island in the middle are known as Browning's Pool and Island after the Victorian poet Robert Browning who lived in Warwick Crescent from 1862 to 1887. The elegant, Regency canalside housing, tree-lined avenues, the willows on Browning's Island with its attendant ducks, geese and swans and the many colourful narrowboats moored here make for a pleasant canal setting. British Waterways' London Canals Office occupies the former toll office at the western entrance to Browning's Pool. Here the canal narrows at a point referred to as Paddington Stop where working boats were stopped, their cargoes gauged and toll tickets issued. Little Venice was the commercial hub of London's canals and was the destination of the famous Paddington Packet Boat horse drawn passenger service inaugurated in 1801 and operating from Cowley Peachey. Today Jason's Trip and the London Waterbus Company run public boat trips from Little Venice. Other attractions include the Puppet Theatre Barge moored here from October to June and the Cascade Floating Art Gallery.

Appropriately Little Venice is the start of the Grand Union Canal Walk at the Junction of Warwick Avenue and Blomfield Road, just a short walk from Warwick Avenue tube station. This is one of the country's newest long distance walks, following the Grand Union Canal towpath for 147 miles (235 km) between Little Venice and Gas Street Basin in the heart of Birmingham.

Covered towpath

Approaching Brentford Gauging Locks heading towards the Thames, the canal and towpath pass through a cavernous warehouse building, now owned by British Waterways but formerly part of Brentford Depot. It was here that cargoes brought up from the London docks on river lighters were transferred to narrowboats bound for the Midlands.

At the adjacent Brentford Gauging Locks barges coming up from the Thames were gauged according to the type and weight of cargo and assessed for tolls. Brentford Gauging Locks and Thames Locks are paired, mechanically operated by the lock-keeper and the canal is partially tidal between them.

Little Venice

| | 0 | 100 | 200 | 300 | 400 yards |
| 0 | 100 | 200 | 300 | 400 metres |

⚠ Thames Lock, number 101, is tidal and passage through it is only possible from 2 hours before High Water in Brentford Creek until 2 hours after between 0600 hours and 2200 hours.

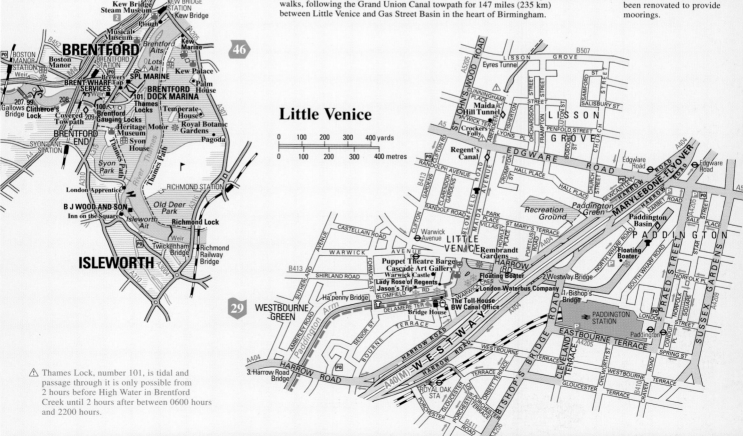

Regent's Canal

Built to provide a canal link with the London Docks, as an alternative distribution route to the River Thames, the 8½ mile (13.5 km) long Regent's Canal opened in 1820 and was largely dependent upon local trade delivering to six major basins - Cumberland, St Pancras, Battlebridge, City Road, Wenlock and Kingsland Basins between Paddington and Limehouse.

Today the Regent's Canal (named like the Park, formerly Marylebone Park, after the Prince Regent) offers some of the most attractive and peaceful urban stretches of canal in Britain. One of the highlights of a journey along it is London Zoo's Northern Aviary, designed by Lord Snowdon, which overlooks the canal. The London Waterbus Company operates public trips from Little Venice to London Zoo to Camden; it is possible to purchase a single or return ticket which includes the entry fee into the zoo.

Maida Hill Tunnel

Maida Hill Tunnel is 272 yards (249 metres) in length and has no towing path. Barges had to be legged through while horses were led over the top. To the east the towpath can be joined from Lisson Grove at Eyres Tunnel.

Spoil from the tunnel excavation was laid over a nearby field which, under the supervision of Thomas Lord who was groundsman to the Marylebone Cricket Club, became Lord's Cricket Ground, home of the MCC since 1814.

Macclesfield Bridge

This bridge is named after the Earl of Macclesfield who was the first chairman of the Regent's Canal Company. It was the scene of a spectacular incident in October 1874 when a boat carrying a cargo of benzol and gunpowder exploded as it was towed under the bridge, after which it has commonly been known as Blow-up Bridge.

The ten original iron supporting columns were salvaged and used to rebuild the bridge but were erected back to front so that today grooves worn by tow ropes appear on both sides of the columns adjacent to the towpath.

Snowdon Aviary, London Zoo, and the Regent's Canal   *Derek Pratt*

⚠ Navigating the tidal Thames should be attempted by experienced boat users in suitably powered and equipped craft. Regulations and details of navigating below Teddington Lock should be obtained from the Port of London Authority in advance of a tidal passage.

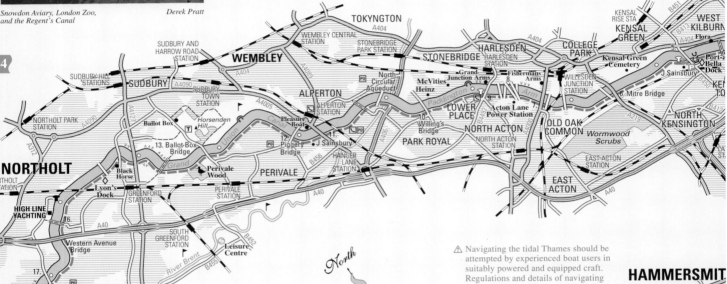

© GEOprojects 1997

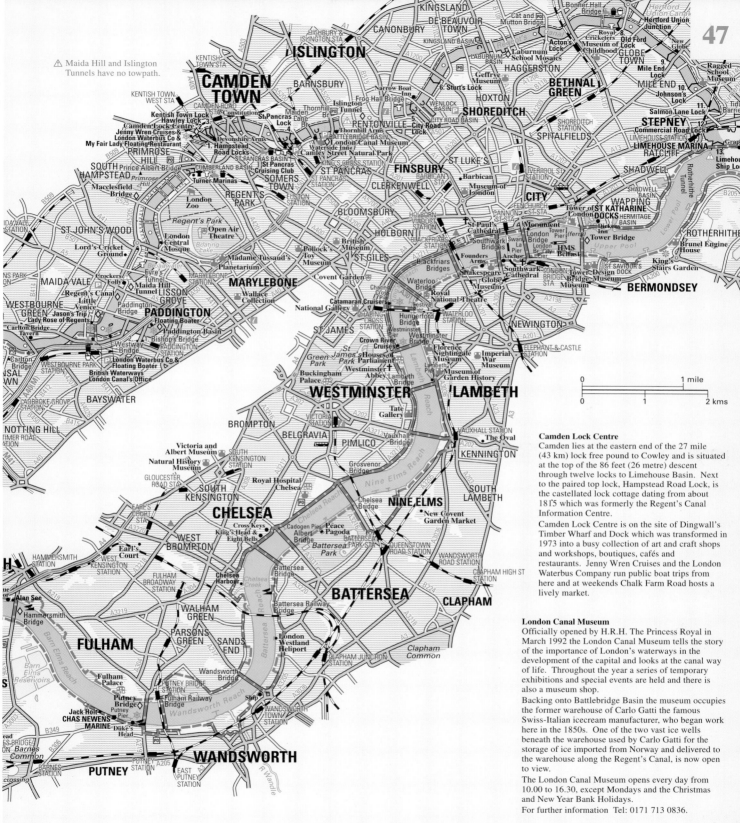

⚠ Maida Hill and Islington Tunnels have no towpath.

Camden Lock Centre

Camden lies at the eastern end of the 27 mile (43 km) lock free pound to Cowley and is situated at the top of the 86 feet (26 metre) descent through twelve locks to Limehouse Basin. Next to the paired top lock, Hampstead Road Lock, is the castellated lock cottage dating from about 1815 which was formerly the Regent's Canal Information Centre.

Camden Lock Centre is on the site of Dingwall's Timber Wharf and Dock which was transformed in 1973 into a busy collection of art and craft shops and workshops, boutiques, cafés and restaurants. Jenny Wren Cruises and the London Waterbus Company run public boat trips from here and at weekends Chalk Farm Road hosts a lively market.

London Canal Museum

Officially opened by H.R.H. The Princess Royal in March 1992 the London Canal Museum tells the story of the importance of London's waterways in the development of the capital and looks at the canal way of life. Throughout the year a series of temporary exhibitions and special events are held and there is also a museum shop.

Backing onto Battlebridge Basin the museum occupies the former warehouse of Carlo Gatti the famous Swiss-Italian icecream manufacturer, who began work here in the 1850s. One of the two vast ice wells beneath the warehouse used by Carlo Gatti for the storage of ice imported from Norway and delivered to the warehouse along the Regent's Canal, is now open to view.

The London Canal Museum opens every day from 10.00 to 16.30, except Mondays and the Christmas and New Year Bank Holidays.
For further information Tel: 0171 713 0836.

Islington Tunnel

At 960 yards (878 metres) Islington is London's longest canal tunnel. There is no towpath and the way over the tunnel is marked by a series of brass plaques set in the pavement. At first barges had to be legged through but in 1826 a steam tug attached to a continuous chain on the canal bed was employed to haul craft through. This it did successfully for over one hundred years being replaced by a diesel tug, no longer in operation, in the 1930s.

Laburnum School Mosaics

The Laburnum School Mosaics brighten the canal scene near the Laburnum Basin which once served the Laburnum Street gas works and is now used for water based recreation activities.

Diagrammatic Section Along the Thames and London Rings

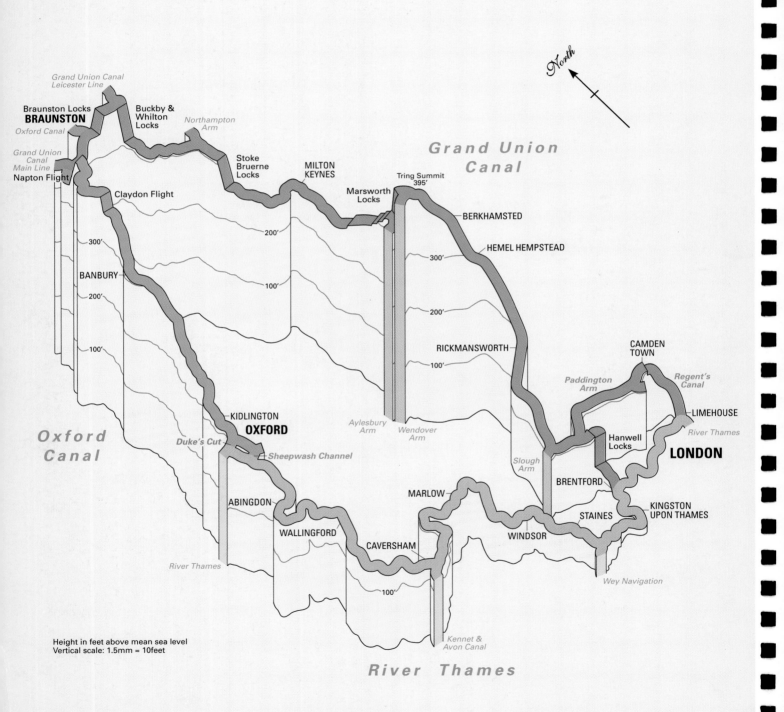

Grand Union Canal
Leicester Line

Braunston Locks
BRAUNSTON

Oxford Canal

Buckby &
Whilton
Locks

Northampton
Arm

Grand Union
Canal
Main Line

Napton Flight

Claydon Flight

Stoke
Bruerne
Locks

MILTON
KEYNES

Marsworth
Locks

Tring Summit
395'

*Grand Union
Canal*

North

BERKHAMSTED

HEMEL HEMPSTEAD

300'

200'

BANBURY

200'

100'

300'

200'

RICKMANSWORTH

100'

100'

CAMDEN
TOWN

Paddington
Arm

Regent's
Canal

LIMEHOUSE

River Thames

KIDLINGTON
OXFORD

Duke's Cut

Sheepwash Channel

Aylesbury
Arm

Wendover
Arm

Hanwell
Locks

LONDON

*Oxford
Canal*

Slough
Arm

BRENTFORD

ABINGDON

MARLOW

STAINES

KINGSTON
UPON THAMES

WALLINGFORD

CAVERSHAM

WINDSOR

River Thames

100'

Wey Navigation

Height in feet above mean sea level
Vertical scale: 1.5mm = 10feet

Kennet &
Avon Canal

River Thames

© GEOprojects 1997